Praise for You Can Ma

≈   ≈   ≈

"A vision that can inspire us to escape the pettiness and failings that divide and limit us. This vision . . . begins with the individual and honors the divine element that is inherent in everyone. Skeele is an experienced guide who writes with clarity and compassion."

—Larry Dossey, MD
Author of *Healing Beyond the Body, Reinventing Medicine,* and
Healing Words
Executive editor of *Alternative Therapies in Health and Medicine*

"A simple, sweet, powerful book about remembering who we are and reconnecting with why we're really here. It's a vital part of humanity's emerging new story."

—Martin Rutte
Coauthor of *Chicken Soup for the Soul at Work*

"A business consultant for over thirty years, I have seen many individuals trapped or imprisoned in a life they would not have chosen. In reading *You Can Make It Heaven*, I have found more than sufficient advice to enable these individuals to begin the journey toward the life they were meant to have."

—Rob Reider
Author of *Operational Review, Benchmarking Strategies,* and
*Improving the Economy, Efficiency, and Effectiveness of
Not-for-Profits*

"Rebecca Skeele's truth, integrity, and inner wisdom guide us to a deeper understanding of life's journey. This book draws the reader to an inner space of reflection and solitude, which creates a greater awareness of one's essential being. It reminds us to more fully connect with the rich threads of our stories, visions, and dreams, to weave a tapestry in our healing journey."

—Barbara Dossey, RN, MS, HNC, FAAN
Author of *Florence Nightingale, Holistic Nursing,*
and *Rituals of Healing*

"Following the principles this book brings forward will surely result in a spirit-filled life of heaven on earth."

—H. Ronald Hulnick, PhD
President of the University of Santa Monica

"Rebecca Skeele offers us a look into the deepest and clearest pond of springwater at her journey to her self. And as we observe, the image sweetly turns into our own. In these pages are precious droplets of rich awakening and a coming home to the divine within."

—Kelle Olwyler
President of Kel Bergan Consulting
Coauthor of *Paradoxical Thinking*

"Personal limitations can become doorways to joy, peace, and inner fulfillment. This is a simple and profound guide, written with humor and practical know-how, to help shift our perspective and create 'heaven' now. We need this kind of guidance today. Beautifully written . . . a book to read again and again."

—Diane Von Welanetz Wentworth
Author of *Send Me Someone*
Coauthor of *Chicken Soup for the Soul Cookbook*

"Heaven is inside us, in our working hands, in our creative imaginations, and in our loving hearts. Rebecca Skeele is a teacher, reminding and coaching the reader that with practice, reeducation, and forgiveness our lives are heaven! The message of this book is precise and practical: happiness, well-being, and success are limitless, and so are we."

—Christina Johnson, MA
Author of *Love Language*

YOU CAN MAKE IT HEAVEN

How to Enrich Your Life
with Abundance
and Loving

REBECCA E. SKEELE

VINCA PUBLISHING, LLC
Santa Fe, New Mexico

You Can Make It Heaven:
How to Enrich Your Life with Abundance and Loving

Published by:
Vinca Publishing LLC
223 N. Guadalupe #701
Santa Fe, NM 87501
www.vincapublishingllc.com

First Edition Published 2002
Editor: Ellen Kleiner
Book design and typography: Diane Rigoli
Cover design: Diane Rigoli
Watercolor mandalas: Michele Faia

Second Edition Published 2019
Book design and typography: Diane Rigoli
Cover Design: Leslie Waltzer
Watercolor mandalas: Michele Faia

Printed in the United States of America

978-0-9715674-1-2 (Keys journal paperback)
978-0-9715674-2-9 (paperback book – second edition)
978-0-9715674-3-6 (mobi)
978-0-9715674-6-7 (epub)

Library of Congress Control Number: 2018967787

This book is lovingly dedicated
to those who blew my heart wide open:

My daughter, Katie
My son, Thomas
My husband, Brian
My teacher, John-Roger

CONTENTS

PART IV: COCREATING WITH YOUR DIVINE NATURE

PART V: SEVEN KEYS TO MAKE YOUR LIFE A HEAVEN

PROLOGUE

Do you often wake up dreading the day ahead? Does your life seem problematic, scary, uncertain, or are things going pretty well but you're secretly waiting for the other shoe to fall? Do hard knocks blow you too easily off course? Does your neighbor, best friend, or coworker get all the breaks? As you stare out the window on your morning commute, does the landscape whizzing by remind you of your daily existence—empty, boring, routine, and purposeless?

There's no need to greet each day in a living hell. Viewing your life differently, you can make it heaven.

For years I had no idea such a transformation was possible. Glued to the treadmill of hectic, mundane living, I was too busy running to notice that I was going nowhere. But when the same emotional dramas surfaced repeatedly, I knew I was in trouble. Ever so gradually I let go of insulting beliefs about myself until, much to my astonishment, I discovered a "me" I never knew existed. It shimmered with potential and seemed to open long-locked doors. So extraordinary was this being that I considered it superhuman, even holy. Before long I did indeed come to know it as a spark of God, and I discovered that this divine spirit resides in everyone.

In my counseling practice over the past decade, I have had the privilege of contemplating many of the knotty ways we humans create hell for ourselves. I have seen how stuck we get in the "story" of our life, letting the past dictate the future and prompting us to say with resignation, "That's the way it is. There's nothing I can do about it." I've noticed how quickly we lash out in self-criticism, putting ourselves down while encouraging and supporting others. I've observed our tendency to devote ourselves exclusively to our children, spouse, parents, or boss, as if our own life purpose were insignificant. Most recently, I've watched feelings of safety and security cave before the horrifying pictures of destruction broadcast into our living rooms.

My clients initially arrive feeling trapped in everything from joblessness to hopelessness, yet divinity eventually announces itself to each one, regardless of their religious or spiritual background. Because it shows up time and again, I have learned to trust in its emergence, to know that given proper circumstances it will reveal itself as a constant source of upliftment, joy, and peace.

We humans have little, if any, prior notion of our divine nature not because it is reclusive or playing hooky, but because we are unable to *see* it. Suffering miserably in a web woven of "failures" and "deficits," we cannot peek between the strands long enough to witness our sparks of light-filled potential. One glimpse, however, and we awaken, as if from a slumber. We begin shaking loose the outgrown past and composing a new future; stepping confidently forward, cherishing our authenticity; delving courageously into previously unexplored realms of self-expression; and uncovering beneath our helplessness, worry, fear, or pain, a loving heart.

I invite you to take this leap of faith with me. Chapter by chapter, dare to trespass the bounds of your known self, in search of hidden sparks within. It is an adventure with no destination, no place of arrival. Instead, walking day by day in increased awareness of your divine nature, you get to grow, hold hands with your truth, and choose accordingly, opening to bigger realities while dispelling false beliefs and delusions of injury, oppression, and defeat. For best results, prepare for awe and wonder.

This book is divided into four parts, each mapping a different segment of the passage. Part I chronicles my own awakening and features a tool to assist in shifting perspective. It sheds light on a simple insight: small miracles that open the heart happen every day, while larger miracles that change lives occur with expanded vision. Part II turns up the bright lights for a look at the many self-imposed obstructions that wreak havoc in human lives. Examples drawn from my clients' experiences reveal the hardships and stalemates caused by perceptions of limitation. Part III presents strategies for gaining liberation from these constraints. Breaking free of perceived limitations, you can find endless possibilities for growth in personal finances, intimacy, career, health, family well-being, community building, and world harmony. Part IV describes keys to cocreation—clues for working in tandem with inner divinity to bring about these transformations. The greatest catalyst for growth is *choosing* to grow, moment by moment, by saying "yes" to the forces of abundance and loving.

Each part of this book opens with a brief prelude and dialogue, and closes with a practice. The dialogues represent student-teacher conversations. Think of the student as the part of you that questions in times of confusion; envision the teacher as the part that sees clearly and understands the "bigger picture." Some people regard this wise orator as a master teacher or guide, an angelic presence or the higher self, *prana* (Sanskrit for "the breath of life") or the divine spark; others conceive of it as the still, small voice of God. Whatever terminology you prefer, imagine the teacher as a benevolent and all-knowing aspect of yourself that wants only the best for you. Deepening your relationship with this genie-in-hiding is sure to enhance your understanding of any quandary that comes to mind. The closing practices take you further, encouraging you to lift the veil and engage your human and divine forces in a sacred, mutually participatory act of cocreation.

As you read this book, make it your own. Apply the ideas that ring true for you and discard those that don't. Adopt the language that suits you and substitute where necessary. Take time between chapters for reflection. Revisit portions as desired, letting them awaken whatever inner forces have yet to unfold. Throughout, stay tuned to the dynamic, alive, ever expanding mystery that is *you*. And don't be surprised if each step of the way, your life suddenly becomes a bit more heavenly.

PART I

Glimpsing New Possibilities

What you are looking for is inside.
What you are seeking is you.

TOP OF IMAGE

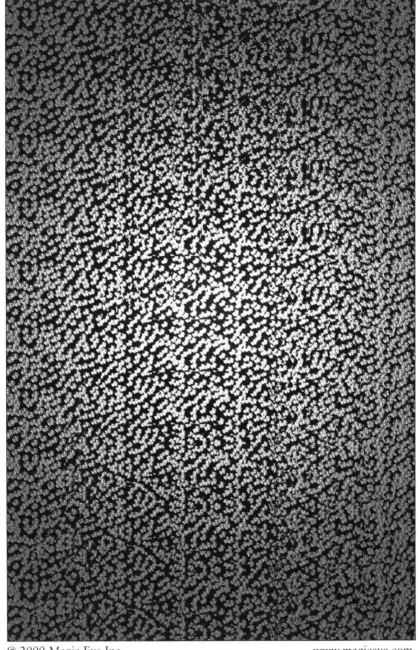

THE MAGIC EYE

Have you ever opened a book of Magic Eye images? If so, you know what it's like to stare at a page of little dots, blinking and wondering, *When am I ever going to see this hidden picture?* Frustrated, you take a deep breath and draw the page closer, then farther away, but still all you see is dots. Only upon softening your gaze and letting your vision become fuzzy do you catch a glimpse of the picture. But invariably you lose it and see only random dots again until refocusing your gaze. After sufficient practice in shifting your focus back and forth from the dots to the picture, you are able to glance at the page, focus easily, and see the image. If you have never had this Magic Eye experience, look for the picture in the dots on page 2.

Seeing the hidden picture demonstrates the potential we have for glimpsing beyond our present beliefs about ourselves, our lives, and the world we live in. Accustomed to our ordinary worldview, we fail to realize that another might exist until circumstances cause us to shift our focus, soften our gaze, and glimpse a new picture of reality. Life presents many such opportunities, each one capable of expanding our worldview to encompass new possibilities.

MAGIC EYE VIEWING INSTRUCTIONS (required for proper viewing): Hold the center of the Magic Eye image *right up to your nose*—it should be blurry. Try not to blink. *Stare* as though you are looking through the image. *Very slowly* move the image away from your face until the 3-D picture comes into focus and the hidden object magically appears! The longer you look, the clearer the object becomes. (For a good look at the hidden object, see page 184.)

Upon seeing a larger picture of reality, do we immediately begin viewing the world this way, abandoning our dot-based perspective? No, because mastering the shift takes patience, practice, guidance, willingness, grace, and a commensurate amount of time. A friend in his fifties, on the verge of refocusing his life, sent me an E-mail alluding to these factors. Although by most standards he "had it all"—years of success in business, property in several states, and a long roster of travels to exotic destinations—he wrote:

> I realize that regardless of appearances to the contrary, I have in essence been a "homeless" person wanting desperately to find a place to belong to. I spent decades focusing on external realities and moving quickly—too quickly—into relationships and structures (businesses, houses, condos), mostly out of fear of being alone. Though this discovery is fairly recent, for an entire year I've been healing the part in me that's afraid of being alone. I had hidden it behind so many masks, and what I concealed most, from myself and others, was my loving. I wanted to share myself but did not know how. Lifting that veil is the essence of these twelve months of my life, and now I'm doing my best to grow.

A Magic Eye experience alone does not ensure growth. In fact, after glimpsing new possibilities for ourselves, we have a choice: we can either remain wedded to our dot-based perspective or, like my friend, set about forging an expanded worldview. Choosing the comfortable and familiar perspective, we know what to expect—more of the same fears, delusions, and cover-ups. Opting for growth, we enter the unknown, encounter hidden parts of ourselves, and compose a more joyous and fulfilling life.

Seeing beyond the dots in my day-to-day existence took me quite by surprise at first, so much so that it shook my world. I had to let go of who I thought I was and what I assumed my life was about. The next four chapters recount defining moments in this shift, illustrating what it's like to awaken to a previously hidden personal truth and begin to build a new life.

THE NATURE OF GLIMPSING

STUDENT: Teacher, the Magic Eye experience now happens at the oddest times. I'll be sitting at my desk stacked with bills to pay, and suddenly I'll see myself at peace with money, no longer worried about shelling out my last dime. But then the picture fades, leaving me more discouraged than before because I couldn't even hold on to the *thought* of making ends meet. Where do these pictures come from?

TEACHER: Perhaps a part of you that is free of worry in such moments is communicating another reality.

STUDENT: Oh, so there's a part of me that wants me to feel terrible about myself.

TEACHER: Quite the opposite. The spark of divinity inside you wants to show you the truth about who you are—the fullness, resourcefulness, and peace you are capable of manifesting.

STUDENT: I would like that experience, but it's not what I'm getting. What's going on?

TEACHER: You're having a revelation of what's possible but your beliefs about yourself won't let you embrace it because your current worldview can't accommodate this understanding.

STUDENT: So, who gave me this worldview?

TEACHER: You did. You've created your perceptions based on the thoughts, feelings, beliefs, and expectations you have of yourself.

STUDENT: Do you mean life isn't something that *happens* to me? I've created it this way *myself?* Well, I don't want to continue creating my life this way. How can I do it differently?

TEACHER: You could try breathing in and breathing out.

STUDENT: I rather thought I *was*. But maybe you're saying I have a choice, and that it's always available, like taking my next breath.

TEACHER: Check it out and see.

STUDENT: Okay, but if I've created these scary perceptions, what should I change them *to?*

TEACHER: Only you know the answer, but you're not yet aware of it. I'd suggest refocusing your eyes and allowing those hidden pictures to come into view more often. Every time you make this choice you will see more of your true self, and little by little those flickering glimpses will give way to a solid experience of who you really are.

STUDENT: And till then I've got to deal with these frustrating intrusions?

TEACHER: As you awaken, the intrusions will fade, much like the pictures do now. You see, revelations of the divine self unfold gradually and always require a decision on your part. Approach each perception of your life with the intention of seeing beyond it and you will deepen your awareness and understanding. Remember, the you that you are seeing is vast. Thus, there is no urgency… Just relax, inhale deeply, and answer the call to turn inward.

CHAPTER ONE

TURNING INWARD

It is rewarding to find someone whom you like, but it is essential to like yourself. It is quickening to recognize that someone is a good and decent human being, but it is indispensable to view yourself as acceptable. It is a delight to discover people who are worthy of respect and admiration and love, but it is vital to believe yourself deserving of these things. For you cannot live in someone else. You cannot find yourself in someone else. You cannot be given a life by someone else. Of all the people you will know in a lifetime, you are the only one you will never leave nor lose. To the question of your life, you are the only answer. To the problems of life, you are the only solution.

— Jo Coudert[1]

Reading these words in 1978, I had a Magic Eye experience. I blinked, reread them, saw myself getting to know the real "me," and thought, *What an odd concept. What good could possibly come from having a relationship with myself?* To my mind at age twenty-seven, this sounded suspect and selfish. Influential people in my southern provincial hometown flashed before my eyes. Did my beloved music teacher know herself? What about the eloquent minister at my church—did he know himself?

Society as I knew it was changing. Women were gathering in meeting places throughout the country, talking about roles, relationships, careers, mothering, their bodies. Nearly all my women friends were intent on sculpting lives different from their mothers'. Many of our husbands were skeptical. Some were hostile. Most kept their thoughts to themselves.

Accustomed to living from the outside in, I identified with the prosperous neighborhood I lived in, my husband's successful business, our standing in the community, and our material wealth. As for my inner world, I expected it to hum along; I'd learned to hold it together no matter what, quickly patching up whatever didn't look good. Well trained in fixing things, I'd become proficient at keeping personal matters under control and running smoothly. So Jo Coudert's words came as a shock. But I liked the picture they inspired, and there awakened within me a gnawing desire to stop obsessing over appearances and start exploring my life from the inside out—getting in touch with my thoughts, feelings, beliefs, expectations, and fears.

Excited and curiously shy, I turned my attention inward to learn how I "ticked." Startled at times by a myriad of anxieties, insecurities, and self-abasing opinions I never knew I had, I would soften my gaze and catch a glimmer of the picture hidden beyond these perceptions. Inadvertently, I launched a seismic shift in my worldview, and with it, a slowly dawning realization that the more my picture of reality expanded, the easier it was to implement change in my life.

Getting to Know Yourself

Today, while it is more socially acceptable to acknowledge our inner terrain, the thought of actually entering it can be just as daunting. For example, my clients never plan to set foot in this territory; rather, they have come up against an obstacle resisting all the gadgets and adhesives at their disposal, and they want help "fixing" their lives. "I'm here because my relationship's coming apart," they will say, or "I want my career decisions mapped out," or "Help me get my partner (spouse, child) back on course," or "I need my body healed, my mind quieted, my fears vanquished."

"What a great opportunity to get to know who you are," I explain gently. "Let's explore your thoughts, feelings, past conditioning, dreams, even the dark places inside, and find out what you're looking for." I pause for feedback.

Some clients smile politely and excuse themselves, never to return. Others ask questions but remain skeptical. Some toy with the idea of turning inward as if fumbling with a box of Cracker Jacks, wondering, *Will the prize inside be worth it?* If their eyes brim with tears and an *aha!* rises from somewhere deep inside, we smile at each other in recognition. Here the journey begins.

But because the inner landscape is one of our last frontiers, doubts quickly surface. *What on earth supports me in looking within? I never learned how to take stock of myself—what if I run into something I can't handle?* People whose loved ones insist that too much introspection is a bad thing soon want to know how to make it a good thing. Still, the adventure seems scary, even dangerous.

At this point, I often recount a two-week rafting trip I took after venturing inward. That summer, I explain, I set off for the Grand Canyon with plans to descend into its innermost recesses and raft the Colorado River. But after visiting the canyon's South Rim and hiking valiantly to the bottom and up again, the thought of rafting through some of the fiercest white water in the Northern Hemisphere began pushing my comfort zone. A voice inside told me the experience would be incredible. Another voice said I was out of my mind—after all, I had to sign a waiver of release in case I didn't make it out alive!

The first morning, the river guides described the dangers, telling our group how to take care of ourselves and one another. They displayed maps showing where we would encounter the white water. Every morning we were briefed on what the day would bring. In some places we could get out of the boats, walk along the shore, and look at the rapids ahead before charting our course. As soon as I realized I was in capable hands, all my fears but one evaporated. The remaining terror—navigating the white water—was something I overcame only by securing my position in the boat and holding on for life.

Journeying inward to get to know who you are is a similar adventure. You will most likely embark with varying degrees of trepidation. While plumbing the twists and turns of the unknown, you'll release these fears. At last you'll meet your hidden self and discover that, perhaps much to your surprise, there is nothing to fix, for nothing is broken. You'll see that your true self is quite whole and capable of dealing with all sorts of difficulties. Using its divine energy to manifest what you most desire, you can then begin constructing a more satisfying life.

Gearing Up

To gear up for the journey inward, you will need three items: a general map of the terrain, a good light, and a competent guide. The terrain you will be exploring is your current worldview—the thoughts, feelings, beliefs, expectations, and fears you harbor based on everything you have experienced until now. Rather than judge any component of your worldview, you will simply observe it. Awareness alone may prompt you to release a perception that no longer serves you. If awareness fails to dissolve it, you can count on a truer perception taking its place the moment you have achieved an expanded sense of who you are.

As for a light, your best illumination will come from your intention to seek the highest truth that can be revealed at that time. Its beam will help you venture beyond the boundaries you are presently accustomed to. The human ego, invested in preserving the "story" of our lives, puts up a fuss when challenged with such new information. But it flees from the bright glow pointing the way to clarity and truth.

Finally, you must enlist a competent guide. You will want to choose carefully from among the many that present you with information. Good guides do not coerce, manipulate, overpower, or proclaim their truth as "the only way." Instead, they continually support you, uplift you, refuse to judge you, and encourage you to confirm all information for yourself. Some guides will approach you from the outside, such as books of all sorts and instructors of one discipline or another. Inside, you have an ever-present guide—a consciousness that urges you on to become who you really are. You can find its voice by working with the dialogues in this book, by asking questions of the wind and other forces of nature, or by inquiring silently or aloud in the shower. If a reply expands your perception of reality, reveals a possibility worth considering, or prompts you to increase your loving toward yourself and others, you can trust it is coming from your inner guide.

With map in hand, your bright light shining, and a reliable guide a breath away, you are equipped to turn safely inward on your adventure. Prepare to unburden yourself of numerous misconceptions and to be pleasantly surprised. Around each bend, a place inside you will open up while another will relax deeply, perhaps for the first time.

CHAPTER TWO

WAKING UP ON IMPACT

I was startled awake from a dream. The house was dark. The glowing red numbers on the bedside clock told me it was very early in the morning. Feeling dread in my stomach, I froze, listening for sounds. No stirrings came from my children's rooms. Relieved, I inhaled deeply, and a voice inside my head whispered, *You have everything you could possibly wish for, but is this all there is to life? Why are you so unhappy? Why don't you wake up every morning excited about what the day will bring?*

Dismissing the strange message, my rational mind countered with, *Why think about such things. You'll only ruin your life. Right now there's nothing wrong with it.*

In my early thirties, unaware that I had reverted to living from the outside in, I would think ahead to the day's activities—a quick swim in the pool, lunch with good friends, a nonprofit board meeting in the afternoon, dinner out with my husband. *The children will be occupied with their nanny, their playmates, and their grandmother, respectively,* I would tell myself. Then I'd sigh and relax. *Yes, I have a fun day planned. My life is great.*

13

But the voice in my head persisted, waking me for weeks with its whispers. Each time, increasingly determined to prove it wrong, I'd grit my teeth and improvise yet another riveting activity for myself. I planned adrenalized vacations sure to stimulate my senses. I shopped compulsively, reveling in the "rush" of spending money. I joined important community organizations and ran philanthropic board meetings, all of which had me feeling worthwhile.

However, the thrill of each binge would quickly wear off. Then I'd look at my world—a happy marriage, two beautiful children, material wealth—and feel a dead place inside, an emptiness I could not understand. *You're supposed to feel wildly happy,* the voice would cry out. *What is wrong with you?*

Early one morning, peering beyond the decorative frame of my life, I saw what was wrong. I had lapsed in my mission to turn inward. My relationship with myself was now skin-deep. The only "me" I knew was a reflection of what I did and what I had. I'd been miming my existence instead of engaging in it. Sitting upright, I envisioned the irritating messages as two-by-four boards whacking me into wakefulness, and I thanked their deliverer for persevering. Little did I know this was just a dress rehearsal.

About a week later, prompted to take stock of my inner perceptions, I came upon a nagging fear that I was not "enough." I saw that in attempting to become something more, I'd turned into an imposter and was terrified of being found out. Hurled into an inner hell, I came face-to-face with a striking paradox: despite having more than enough material possessions, I was plagued by a deep sense of lack, leading me to overspend and overindulge. An accompanying sense of guilt about this excessive materiality had me feeling responsible for everyone and everything. But the harder I tried to please others so as not to be perceived as a rich snob, the more disgust I felt toward me. *Who am I?* I asked myself, on the verge of throwing up. *What do I want out of life?*

Hell soon thickened. Friends I shared my inner turmoil with said, "Get over it. What you have should be enough." Privately I agreed, berating myself not only for wanting something more but also for complaining. My head throbbed with pain as I concluded that I did not *have* a problem, I *was* the problem.

Fortunately my inner prompter intervened: *Stop making yourself wrong about your thoughts and feelings. Instead, consider that your discontent, worry, and fear are really personal truths knocking at your door.* Taking this advice to heart, I allowed for my agitation, stopped identifying myself as the problem, and little by little glimpsed my way out of hell.

To make sure I remained attentive, other two-by-fours followed. My husband's prosperous business declared bankruptcy, bringing up fears of financial collapse. Our family relocated hundreds of miles from the provincial southern town I'd known all my life, forcing me to relinquish my status as an outstanding community member. My outer support network of friends and family fell away, and I had no clue how to find an inner one. The illusion of my happy marriage crumbled, giving way to self-judgment. To generate an income, I entered the work force, running an office for a nonprofit organization, but I had little confidence in my abilities. The future seemed scary, dark, and suffocating.

Life as I knew it had disintegrated, and along with it, my identity. My options were clear: I could either choke amidst the rubble all around me or, using the Magic Eye technique, look inside for a new view of this mess. As for the two-by-fours, I could continue to let them whack at me or I could awaken to their knocks. Mustering whatever courage, strength, patience, and clear intention I could, I shook myself awake and turned my gaze inward. There I uncovered doubts about my capacity to love and be loved, insecurity about my talents and abilities, and a lack of self-esteem. To construct a life that worked, I obviously needed to get unstuck from one that didn't, so I searched more deeply and gradually found firmer pieces of an inner "me." Inching my way out of the debris, I made a solemn commitment: in the future I would scrupulously follow my body's cues of discomfort and patiently await the emergence of deeper truths.

Body Wisdom

When the mind falls asleep on the job of turning inward, we can count on the body to wake us up. A startle reflex here, an emptiness or fluttering there—all signal the presence of a deeper message awaiting our attention. If we override the subtle cues, more tumultuous ones emerge from the shadows, letting us know that one of life's two-by-fours is at the door to the inner self. Ignore the knock and it may only return, louder and more irritating than before. Answer it and we have an opportunity for discovery and growth.

Life as we know it is often interrupted. At such times, which tend to be embarrassing if not outright messy, the mind bids us to endure the situation or fix it or hurry up and get through it. The body, less defended, knows better. It will have us feeling out of sorts at first, or out of sync. Over time it may manifest aches, chronic pains, even panic attacks. Ultimately we realize that the body, in its profound wisdom, is our best interpreter. Deciphering two-by-four interruptions as growth-promoting opportunities, it relays increasingly amplified sensations to capture our attention.

To experience body wisdom for yourself, read through the following descriptions of major two-by-fours. If you have undergone any of these life disruptions and grown from them, your body may not respond at all. If you have more to discover from them your body will send you a message.

Divorce. The breakup of a marriage shatters dreams and dissolves beliefs in a "happily ever after" relationship. Shaking the core of the family unit, it destroys the fabric of love, commitment, and trust.

Financial collapse. Bankruptcy, loss of a job, forfeiture of a house, or depleted investments threaten personal and family security. With no apparent source of income, a person feels unsafe and afraid. Survival becomes paramount; self-esteem suffers.

Debilitating illness. Disease invites intimations of mortality and of the transient nature of life itself. Too ill to move fluidly through the course of a day, a person feels resentful, perhaps betrayed, viewing the body as an enemy.

Depression. Clouds of depression evoke feelings of sadness and discouragement, an inability to think clearly or concentrate, and a sense of exhaustion, increasing the need for sleep. Days, though busy, seem dull and lifeless. Severe depression leads to withdrawal, an intractable sense of hopelessness, and suicidal feelings.

Loss of a loved one. Death of a loved one arouses overwhelming feelings of anger, helplessness, and grief. Instances of sudden tragedy up the ante, giving way to obsessive feelings of abandonment, rage, the unfairness of life, and wanting to "even the score." A person in this state can find no peace.

Addictions. Physical compulsions and mental obsessions pertain to almost anything—illegal drugs, alcohol, food, sex, work, exercise, smoking, medications, gambling, television, computers, control, perfection, rage, and much more. Persistent reliance on habit-forming activities promotes feelings of desperation, futility, dejection, and despair. Agitation is another constant companion, for never is there enough "elixir" to quiet the mind. The death-defying recklessness eventually engenders a downward-spiraling sense of defeat, loss of faith, and loss of heart.

Insomnia. The inability to obtain adequate sleep manifests in overly heightened reactions to minor irritations, poor judgment, and globalized anxiety. Sleep debt also leads to absenteeism from work, as well as driving and job-related accidents. Prolonged sleep deprivation can negatively affect physical health as well.

Lack of purpose. Stumbling blindly through each weekday and drifting through weekends wears away at human resolve. Decision making falters, intentions and goals evaporate, and a pervasive sense of powerlessness takes over. Life becomes a series of hit-or-miss events, appearing arbitrary, or worse, meaningless.

Who's That Knocking at Your Door?

Physiological responses to a life event, no matter how justifiable they may seem in light of the turbulence, indicate there's a two-by-four urging us into wakefulness. Disregarding these sensations, we may continually experience the disabling aftereffects of the calamity we have suffered, ignorant of our true selves and therefore trapped in self-sabotaging behaviors. The other option is take heed of the sensations and see what part of us is wanting to emerge and help us reconstruct our lives.

If your body gave you feedback as you read through the description of two-by-fours, you might be living in the shadow of that past event, still asleep to parts of your essence. Fortunately two-by-fours persevere, so it is never too late to wake up on impact and glimpse the secret part of you that's knocking at your door. The message is sure to answer any number of questions: Who are you now, as opposed to then? What thoughts or feelings about yourself might be hampering your ability to live a fruitful life? What beliefs about yourself might be restricting your capacity to experience joy? What fears stand in your way?

In answering the knock at your door, you can shatter all the illusory perceptions governing parts of your life that don't work, meet the real you, and together draft a blueprint of the life you want. For a new perspective on these two-by-fours, take a breath, soften your focus, and read on.

Divorce. The breakup of a marriage shatters pipe dreams about romantic love and unrealistic expectations about "till death do us part." It also dissolves the notion that another person makes us happy and whole. When the wounds of divorce initiate a journey of self-discovery, they pave the way to a deeper understanding of commitment, trust, relationships, and family. Journeying forth, we find that love—the essence of who we are—is available to us in every moment.

Financial collapse. Bankruptcy, or the loss of a job, account, house, or investments, bursts the bubble of safety whirled by material possessions. Finding no sanctuary in a lifestyle fashioned on something so ephemeral as money, we detach from finance-driven distractions and compulsions, only to discover that true security lies within. Turning inward, we come upon the one enduring treasure: the self.

Debilitating illness. Mortality is a powerful teacher. It corrodes the bedrock of any belief system that identifies the human being as merely a physical organism. Beyond the flesh, we uncover a fount of wisdom emanating from the core of our being. As we expand our awareness in this direction, we encounter the divine spark within us.

Depression. Hiding from the world to escape the pain of unresolved memories and feelings is like entering a cavern of long-frozen emotions. Expressing and releasing them, we set free entire chunks of our essence, greeting each one with acceptance, forgiveness, and loving. Amidst the melting of these glacial drifts, we befriend our wholeness.

Loss of a loved one. Despair following the death of someone dearly beloved eclipses all light, within and without. Choosing to live, perhaps for the first time, we walk steadfastly through the darkness. When we reclaim our stake in life, we emerge into daylight cleansed, expanded, and renewed.

Addictions. The deadening forces of addiction reveal that no fix can once and for all counteract the sense of starvation that leads to cravings. To the contrary, bingeing distances us further from real sources of nourishment—our innermost feelings, our connections with other people, and the divine spark within us. When recovery guides us back to the deepest parts of the self, which the addiction has obscured, a sense of fullness and knowingness at last silences the voice of longing, turning our defeats into victories.

Insomnia. Sleeplessness summons us to confront our greatest spooks. Facing a beast that comes out only in the dark sheds light on this previously unconscious fear. Then in the beam of our awareness it vanishes, like the bogeyman. No longer is it menacing, for it has joined our expanding pool of self-knowledge.

Lack of purpose. Purposelessness keeps us stalled at the shaft to a huge mine of forgotten hopes and dreams. Unable to move forward, we begin peeling away the slabs of hurt and disappointment that block the entryway. Dislodging these obstructions, we restore our energy and enthusiasm, and in time we unearth the precious ore that is ours alone.

Life's two-by-fours are great awakeners, capable of catalyzing unparalleled insights. On initial impact they can easily hurl you back into sleep, for you may be too fraught with pain, fear, resentment, anger, or upset to find any value in them. It takes considerable courage, and often years, to go beyond the hurt of a trauma. But timing does not matter. What counts is waking up to answer a recurring knock, for then you begin to transform your life.

CHAPTER THREE

HEARTFELT DEFINING MOMENTS

Keeping my commitment to remain aware of inner states, I attended a personal growth seminar in my mid-thirties. Early in the six-day workshop the facilitator launched into a description of "weevily" peanuts. She cupped her hands in front of her, filled with imaginary peanuts, and solemnly explained that a weevil is a small beetle that lives off of live or harvested crops. She demonstrated how we take very good care of our ravaged peanuts, rationing them out to ourselves one at a time. This is what sustains us, she stated. We settle for our lot in life. We protect and defend the constricted, stress-ridden reality we call our existence, every day thinking, *This is it. This is all my life will ever be. I must take care of it.*

I was appalled. Silently I grumbled, *What do you mean my life is like weevily peanuts? Do you realize how hard I have worked? How good I have been? Who I am?*

As I sat stewing in my resistance, tears filled my eyes and I thought, *The aching in my heart has been the truth all along. I don't really let others in. I don't really know how to love myself or anyone else. My hard work and good behavior are meant to please others, because my happiness depends on their favorable opinions of me. I don't know who I am, and that scares me.*

The facilitator went on to describe the "banquet table of life." She opened her arms wide to show the vastness of the spread. This table, she said, is laden with every delicious food we can imagine. People are eating, laughing, and enjoying themselves. The banquet table of life represents all manner of abundance, every delicacy our hearts desire. If we imagine it in our lives, it appears. If we hunger for its riches, we need only partake. The banquet table of life fulfills our every want and need to perfection.

As she described the magnificent banquet table, I could see it in my mind. Much like entering a Magic Eye experience, I suddenly beheld this larger way of living, this glimpse of heaven. I wanted to bolt for the door. *This is too much. Don't show me the promised land and tempt me into believing I could actually arrive,* I thought. Biblical legends, fairy tales, and wisdom stories funneled into my awareness. I became every mythical hero and heroine who had ever stood transfixed by a glimpse of the Holy Grail yet felt unworthy of having it. I stared into the gaping hole I called my heart and wept. How I longed to trade in my weevily peanuts, one by one, for a sumptuous banquet.

When our hearts are touched by the vision of new possibilities, they spark a powerful defining moment, spurring on our first steps toward expansion. Such moments open us to inner guidance and rekindle deep, unspoken yearnings. Whether acted upon or tucked away for later illumination, these glimpses are easily recalled years in the future.

I often ask people to identify defining moments in their lives. Here are three accounts, each reflecting an accompanying awareness that the person's life was about to change forever.

The following story illustrates how a defining moment can occur in the course of everyday life.

In my mid-forties, after the breakup of a significant relationship, I went into a place of deep healing. I studied *A Course in Miracles,* listened to self-growth tapes, did a lot of soul-searching, and tried to come to terms with the relationship. I wanted to know what my life was about and where was I going.

One day I went on a bike ride in my neighborhood, something I frequently did. This time, as I turned onto a residential street that was usually very busy, I heard a voice say, *Focus on the pavement. Do not look ahead. Be present to where you are. Trust and the way will unfold.* I had heard the voice off and on for years, but never was its counsel so foolhardy. At first I argued, *This is nuts. How can I be safe if I don't watch where I'm going?* The message came again, and curiously receptive, I followed its bidding.

I looked at the pavement and focused on the center stripe. It was frightening not to see where I was going, but fortunately there was little traffic. After about three blocks the voice said, *Turn left,* and I thought, *Oh my God, can I do this?* I couldn't trust myself to turn without looking ahead, so I glanced up just long enough to see a delivery truck double-parked down the street. I quickly refocused on the pavement, thinking, *Well, it's a good thing I looked. I could have stormed into the back of that truck!* Just before I reached the truck, a sudden noise made me look up. I smiled, realizing that if I had not peeked earlier, I still would have seen the truck in time.

I rode on with a bit more confidence. A few minutes later I heard the voice say, *Turn left.* I turned and saw peripherally that I was on one of the busiest boulevards in town. I rode along without looking up, then again I heard, *Turn left.* Soon I was riding against traffic. Once more I heard, *Turn left,* which I did, and thus my ride continued until I found myself back home.

I marveled at this experience. I had been perfectly safe throughout, and my one need to exert control had proved unnecessary. In fact, the more I surrendered to the instructions, the freer I was to enjoy the ride.

The next day I set off again on my bike. A few blocks down the road I heard, *This time, no hands. You need not direct your way.* Riding with no hands was something I envied my brothers for doing yet had never accomplished myself. I nervously did as instructed. After a few wobbles I was able to ride in and out of driveways, over root-raised sidewalks, across gravel, down busy streets, and around parked cars. Once again I arrived home unscathed. Once again I was not in control of the ride. I was clearly being protected.

Later that day I wrote on a card: "Remember the bicycle ride. Be present and focused, and trust. The way will unfold." I kept the card on my bathroom mirror for years, reading it whenever I felt lost, afraid, or unsure of where I was going. Recalling the biking experience, I would immediately calm down. And so I have developed a deep sense of trust. Occasionally I'll experience fear or doubt, but beneath it, in the center of my heart, there's trust.

The bicycle rides were defining moments for me. They awakened trust in the guidance that is always with me. They showed me the importance of paying attention to the "now" and knowing the future will unfold on its own. Those bike rides became a metaphor for my life.

Sometimes the defining moment takes place on a spiritual retreat.

For weeks I had been plagued with a nagging sense of unrest. Taking a hiatus from work, I visited a local monastery for rest and reflection. I felt replenished but still didn't know what was wrong. One morning while meditating in the back of the simple church, I heard a voice inside my head say, *It's about God.* My heart seemed to melt open, and I instinctively knew the truth of those words. My inner crisis was about my relationship with Spirit, which I had put on hold to live my life. Every atom of my body responded with recognition, and I wept with joy. That moment changed the course of my life.

A defining moment can also arise while envisioning an ideal situation.

Teaching had been my passion for years. However, I was exhausted at the end of each school day and longed for a life outside of work. One evening I decided to envision an ideal day. Closing my eyes, I saw myself no longer teaching in the cold northern climate where I lived but painting outdoors in the high desert of the Southwest. I shrugged the picture off, repelled by the thought of leaving my friends, our community, and my devotion to teaching. *Close your eyes and look again,* chirped a voice in my head. *This is your future.* I did as directed, and something in my core opened like a rosebud. A thrill rushed through me at the prospect of a life that far exceeded my hopes and dreams.

Perhaps you have turned inward and awakened to one of life's galvanizing knocks. But did you follow the instructions of your inner voice, and did you feel something shift in your heart? Whereas life's traumatic two-by-fours can awaken the psyche, defining moments stir the heart, releasing spiritual forces that move us toward a deeper truth. They answer an easily denied cry for direction with an undeniable picture of it.

Interestingly, the rational mind has little success in "arranging for" a defining moment. The stage for these appearances is set not by thoughts, concepts, or even convictions, but by attentiveness to inner stirrings, for defining moments are pure creations of the divine spark within. You will know you are in the midst of one if you receive a message that engages your heart, transporting you beyond your comfort level, fears, worries, or concerns. You will feel its energy at work while bringing new perceptions to old pastimes, or while integrating an awe-inspiring activity into your day, or taking a leap of faith. To prepare for a defining moment's debut, keep open the door to your inner world, aware that your heart, seemingly unbeckoned, may present you with an unforeseen possibility and announce that your worldview is about to shift radically.

CHAPTER FOUR

THE POWER OF CHOICE

. . . so that when
we finally step out of the boat . . .
we find
everything holds
us, and everything confirms
our courage, and if you wanted
to drown you could,
but you don't
because finally
after all this struggle
and all these years
you don't want to any more
you've simply had enough
of drowning
and you want to live and you
want to love . . .

—from "THE TRUELOVE"
by DAVID WHYTE[1]

While reading this verse several years ago, I bolted to attention. I had put the pieces of my life back together, but still it lacked luster, still I felt joyless. After all the struggles and insights, I seemed to be holding tightly to a familiar bulwark, as if floating endlessly in the little boat on the Colorado River. I understood where I had been in my life but had no idea where I was going. Safety and security had won out over the banquet table of life, leaving me directionless.

Control was paramount. My inner controller, as alert as a firefighter, stood shovel in hand to clear away any fallout from old beliefs that came tumbling down. To prevent disruption from new insights, Mr. Firefighter extinguished all sparks that seemed the least bit out of the ordinary. Staying in control had become a full-time job.

Then, too, there was the disturbing persistence of old patterns. Although aware of a small yet commanding truth deep inside me, I was afraid of not being at the right place at the right time, not measuring up, not looking good, and being considered a fool. Newly divorced, I worried incessantly about being abandoned by everyone I knew, and left alone. I was a self-proclaimed victim of circumstance, certain that life would "happen to me" no matter what precautionary measures I might take. *Yes*, I told myself, *it is definitely time to step out of this boat.*

As was customary, my inner prompter urged me on, saying, *You are the sum total of choices you have made, so if you want different results you'll have to make different choices.*

The awareness that I could actually choose my circumstances dawned slowly, a flicker at a time. Accepting that I was about to become very uncomfortable, I listened more closely to my inner guide. But the message was not reassuring. *Go where you don't want to go!* he commanded. Although stunned, I knew I would follow the dictates of an expanded yet not fully tested part of me—my heart. *Are you crazy?* roared Mr. Firefighter, offended at losing his job. *You'll fall prey to emotional overwhelm. Sparks are sure to fly, billowing rapidly into blazes.*

Ever so gradually I stepped out of my cozy vessel and propelled myself into uncharted waters. I trembled at the thought of facing scary parts of myself—worries, fears, self-judgments, doubts, and long-held beliefs—yet I felt inwardly guided and more than ready to embark on a fulfilling life. Moved on by the power of choice, I knew at last that I could never turn back.

Making Different Choices

Choice is critical to change. It unleashes the energy that turns dreams into realities. But most people, including those who have seen how bountiful their lives can be, tend to resist change. Soon they slide into "autopilot" in their careers and their relationships. Eventually many idle into paralysis, ceaselessly reenacting hardships rooted in the same nagging fears, worries, or pains they have always known.

Aware of your potential for a better life, you may be drifting along and wondering why. Or you may be confused about how to live your life differently, or what it might require. Choosing to take a first step despite uncertainties can lift you out of your self-defeating holding patterns. As my inner prompter so wisely advised: If you want different results, you'll have to make different choices.

Of the more than 90,000 thoughts vying for your attention over the course of any day, growth-promoting choices are among them and are necessary to further your expansion. Following are several that can keep you moving forward by strengthening your connection with your inner guide.

Choose to honestly take stock of your life. Knowing *where* you are and *who* you are can give you a baseline to use in surveying the future. To take stock, ask yourself a few questions, such as: "How do I feel waking up in the morning?" "How much energy do I invest in acquiring material possessions and tending to outer appearances?" "What is my current mission in life?" "Am I at peace?" "Who am I anyway?"

Choose to pay attention to whatever is not working in your life. Once you understand what keeps getting in your way, you can break free of it. To gain perspective, ask yourself: "What recurring scenario in my life would I rather avoid?" "What's most upsetting at home, on the job, and in my social interactions?" "What do I do to feel safe and secure?" "Are these measures enhancing my sense of joy and fulfillment?" "What might happen if I give them up?" As always, you will need to look at what you least want to see—your feelings of inadequacy, fears of failure, and lack of trust.

Choose to examine your relationships. Your interactions with others can either support or dismantle your sense of belonging; they also reflect how you feel about *yourself*. Here are some questions to ponder: "What sorts of people am I drawn to?" "What types of social situations do I shy away from?" "Do I close off communication with certain people?" "What do I judge about them that also might be true of me?" "Are my connections with people open channels for giving and receiving love?" Use your answers to identify attitudes, numb spots, and emotional shut-downs that are impeding fulfillment in your relationships.

Opting for a More Loving Relationship with Yourself

Your relationship with yourself is the determining factor in shaping a more fulfilling future. The reason is that in befriending yourself, you get to embrace your divine nature—the knowing spark within that alone can move you from glimpsing new realities to manifesting them. Your divine nature is your secret collaborator, your ever-present guide through hardships, and your partner in creating heaven. Together, you excavate and cocreate.

Here, in her words, is how one of my clients developed a more loving relationship with herself.

In October 1998, I didn't want to live anymore. My marriage was falling apart, debilitating headaches made me ill, and I was numb from painkillers and antidepressants. I woke up each morning feeling hopeless and unable to find joy in anything, including my two children.

My husband and I had recently separated, and he'd insisted on keeping our children for half of each week. So when they were home with me, from Saturday night to Wednesday morning, I held my life together; from Wednesday through Saturday, I fell apart. To escape my misery I slept—between ten and twelve hours a night, with intermittent morning and afternoon naps. The highlight of each day was watching the video *The Little House on the Prairie* while eating lunch.

Looking back, I can see how I might have descended into such a miserable abyss. After my separation, my best friend deserted me and began dating my husband; they are now engaged to be married. Most of my other friends stopped calling and dropping by. I probably hadn't been such a good friend to them. People thought of me as "distant," "a loner," and "independent." I had counted on my husband to initiate and organize our social activities. I had no career or meaningful work, and lacked the energy to pursue community involvement. Then, too, my father was dying from cancer.

One evening a friend gave me the phone number of a spiritual counselor she was working with. At the end of my rope, I decided to call. During our conversation, the counselor asked if I could commit to making a change in my life. "Yes," I said, certain that without taking action I would soon die.

Very gently, over the course of many sessions, my counselor introduced me to someone very important: my self. Accepting the presence of a divine spirit within me took some doing. I had been reared as a Southern Baptist in a small Texas town. I had learned strict rules and felt guilty every time I broke them. We were not taught to love ourselves, much less *know* ourselves. Nor would I have wanted to since I was sure there were lots of bad forces inside me. More than anything else, I was full of self-hatred.

With the counselor's help I slowly began to reclaim my self and set forth on a path to self-love. The journey was painful, scary, confusing, challenging, fascinating, and beautiful.

Now, more than two years later, I am pain free and unmedicated. I understand there is no greater gift than self-love and that my spirit wants this for me. I am creating a life suffused with love and happiness. I cherish my new career in massage therapy, and my future looks exciting. I'm making terrific friends. I have a wonderful relationship with my children—we laugh a lot and spend evenings dancing around the house to our favorite music.

My life isn't perfect. My ex-husband and I are battling in court over finances. I don't have my children as often as I'd like. My former friends don't understand me, and few support my choices—some of which are pretty risky since I push the envelope a little. But I've learned that what happens *inside* me is what makes my life work. When I listen to my spirit, I am happy.

In befriending ourselves we experience deep happiness. The more we tell ourselves the truth, the more we shrink the places inside that want to believe lies. When we start the day by greeting our reflection in the mirror with love instead of reproach, we brighten and enlighten our surroundings.

The power of choice emits that shine. It will begin to cast its glow for you as soon as you say "yes" to loving yourself. This can occur in the depths of survival time, as it did for my client, when the pain inside is causing illness and there is no option but to change. It can happen when, tired of punishing yourself with a demoralizing worldview adopted long ago, you decide to lighten up. A glimmer might even appear when, disenchanted by neon lures, you begin to search for a more enduring reality. Whenever your inner truth captures your attention, despite trepidation over what might lay ahead, rejoice . . . it is a happy day.

PRACTICE

Heaven Is . .

Most notions of heaven refer to the afterlife. Here you will concentrate on *this* life, capturing impressions left by special objects you have seen, or images portrayed in books, movies, or paintings; discarding those you have outgrown; and inviting input from your inner teacher. Clearing out the old makes way for the new.

PART I

᭡ Across the top of an 8 1/2-by-11-inch sheet of paper, write, "Heaven is . . ." Complete this sentence as many times as you wish, jotting down images that flash through your mind. Include as much detail as possible.

᭡ Next, think deeply about each image, then delete those that are no longer relevant. For example, if you described heaven as a place with puffy white clouds at the top of a long staircase reserved for dead football players—as in the film *Heaven Can Wait*—but you do not currently envision heaven with puffy white clouds and football players, delete this item.

᭡ Beside each remaining item, note the feelings it evokes within you. For instance, if you wrote, "Heaven is a shiny red sports car," describe what it would be like to drive this car. If you wrote, "Heaven is a mutually loving, supportive partnership," describe how you would feel in this relationship.

PART II

- Take a deep breath, close your eyes, and ask your inner teacher, "What is heaven?"

- Next, imagine that you are facing a large movie screen. Continuing to breathe deeply and calmly, allow whatever images arise to slowly appear on the screen. Make a mental note of your experience before opening your eyes.

- On a second sheet of paper draw this new glimpse of heaven, or portray it in words or symbols.

- Write today's date on both sheets of paper and file them for safekeeping.

Our birth is but a sleep and a forgetting:
The soul that rises with us, our life's star,
Hath had elsewhere its setting,
And cometh from afar:
Not in entire forgetfulness,
And not in utter nakedness,
But trailing clouds of glory do we come
From God,
Who is our home:
Heaven lies about us in our infancy!

—WILLIAM WORDSWORTH[2]

PART II

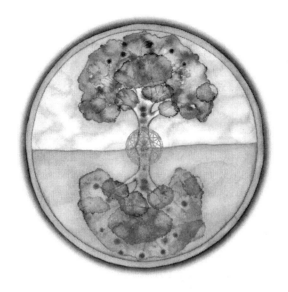

Recognizing
Self-Limitations

*We see the world not as it is
but as we are.*

TURNING ON THE BRIGHT LIGHTS

Most people who have chosen to explore the dark terrain inside are astonished by what they see. Gnarled thoughts and feelings about themselves block their forward vision; tangled beliefs and expectations form a canopy overhead; and around every bend there lurks a fear. Some adventurers stop here, mistaking these misshapen forms for the true self. Others turn on their bright lights and, less influenced by conclusions drawn earlier in life, perceive that their true essence lies further on. They also know that to get there they must traverse the difficult landscape before them, reexposing themselves to long-familiar experiences of pain, separation, fear, and self-doubt.

All of us are beset by misunderstandings from our past. With repeated appearances they seem to confirm our limited understanding of who we are, keeping our worldview constricted and hindering our ability to lead bountiful lives. These self-limitations run the gamut from either-or thinking and negative mind-sets to crippling beliefs and responses. But recognize them we must, for then our perspective begins to shift, enabling us to not only *see* the truth but come to *know* it.

The following chapters explore some of the most common ways in which we limit ourselves. You will read about people encountering these aspects of themselves and pressing beyond them. All the while, you might recognize some of your own tendencies. If so, acknowledge them. Then seeing them as dots on a page, soften your gaze and shift your focus to glimpse the truth hidden in the background.

Once you are aware of them, some limited perceptions will simply fall away like a suit that no longer fits. Others may be more tenacious. Fortunately the goal is not to be completely free of limited perceptions but to explore beyond them, viewing yourself from a truer, more encompassing vantage point. See yourself as dwarfed and you will believe you are; turn up the lights to experience your fullness and that is what you will create. Each step of the way treat yourself with kindness.

THE NATURE OF SELF-LIMITATION

STUDENT: Teacher, please talk to me about self-limitation. A part of me is reluctant to explore how I diminish myself. I'm afraid of getting caught in the distortions and losing my way.

TEACHER: You cannot get lost when you are on a path of self-discovery. All such paths lead to the understanding that human experience is but a piece of a greater experience that is happening beyond the mind's limited perceptions.

STUDENT: But it's so easy to believe that this body, this room, this chair, this computer, and the air I am breathing is all there is. There's a part of me that stubbornly accepts this reality and no other.

TEACHER: I understand. Yet your awakening is as predictable as the larva that will become a butterfly. The transition from caterpillar to cocoon to butterfly is a natural unfolding. Your awakening beyond self-limitation is just as natural. Everything has its divine timing.

STUDENT: Do I have to go through as many stages as the butterfly? Frankly, I'd rather skip that middle one and say, "I'll pass. I don't want to be this cocoon right now."

TEACHER: The cocoon is the butterfly in a very real sense. When it is ready, and not one second sooner, it breaks open and the butterfly emerges. But it will take time for the butterfly to know the fullness of its experience as a winged creature. Revelation requires many levels of awakening.

STUDENT: So if I regard my self-limitations as a cocoon stage, then I can trust that when I am fully ready they will drop away and something new will emerge?

TEACHER: Yes, and remember the part of you that is already the winged butterfly. The spark of divine consciousness deep inside you created the potential for your every unfolding.

STUDENT: So parts of me are becoming a butterfly, while other parts are already a butterfly? And still other parts are something else entirely? Are you saying the caterpillar on some level knows what it is becoming and that I can know what I am becoming?

TEACHER: The caterpillar becomes what it must. Until then, it is both a butterfly and a butterfly-in-the-making. You will become what you must—an awakened consciousness cocreating with the divine. Until then, you are both an awakened, cocreative consciousness and one-in-the-making. Enjoy the transformation. It's all been designed in perfection.

CHAPTER FIVE

LIFE-STORY TREASURES
AND TRAPS

Life stories are repositories of self-limitations, and therefore ideal starting points for expanding our awareness. Each of us has a life story, a narrative woven of our successes, failures, losses, disappointments, epiphanies, wake-up calls, and defining moments. It holds, in little freeze-frames, the primary themes of our existence—poignant events that have happened to us and, in the best circumstances, our responses.

Telling this story can promote healing and growth. Storytelling circles meeting in church basements, living rooms, or coffee shops offer countless people the chance to feel connected with others—to share and be heard, understood, and purified. While telling our life story in any ambiance of acceptance, we glean new wisdom from the tapestry of our lives. We also find strength to intertwine the loose strands of a devastating loss, abuse, or a life-threatening illness. With the warp and woof complete, we embrace our story and move on.

But too often our story engulfs us. All we can see are its headlines, which we tell over and over, giving no thought to their meanings. These skimpy headlines define our worldview, giving rise to a myriad of immobilizing thoughts, feelings, beliefs, and self-defeating behaviors.

Signs of engulfment are easy to spot. We meet someone for the first time and they ask: "What do you do for a living?" "Tell me about your family," "What's the weather like in Columbus?" "Do you enjoy raising children?" We reply with ease, happy to be in the realm of the known, delighted to impart the contours of our existence. But spend time chatting beyond the banners and a few captions, and traces of the story begin to emerge. Somewhere between "What do you do for a living?" and "What was it like then?" out come one-liners bearing the insignia of untapped themes, such as these:

"I was raised in the South."

"My family had money."

"My father was an alcoholic."

"I was adopted."

"I've been divorced."

"I'm a single mom."

"I'm a stepfather."

"My mother died when I was a child."

"I'm a third-generation Hispanic (African, Asian, Arab) American."

Our inner chorus, dedicated to the preservation of comfort, intervenes, howling:

I knew she would be displeased when I said that.

I wonder what he thinks about me now.

That was a dumb thing to blurt out.

Men always say that.

Women are such name-droppers.

Stay away from this person. They have that "look."

At this point, the conversation can easily veer off into sports, world events, or the latest traffic jam. But a more growth-promoting choice is to override the chorus of censors and begin extending our comfort zone.

Peering Beneath the Headlines

Casual conversations are perfect occasions for peering beneath the surface of a life story. Considerable self-knowledge can be gleaned by pausing in midsentence to find the meaning of our last statement. For example, we might ask ourselves:

Why that quip about being divorced? What are my beliefs about marriage?

What am I really communicating by saying I'm a single mom?

Does the chronic pain in my lower back, which throbs at each mention of my mother's death, have anything to do with old, unexpressed anger?

Do I see myself compromised by my birthplace, career, family, social status, or painful past?

What would my life look like now if I had taken more responsibility for choices earlier?

Do I have two drinks every night because my folks did?

Why don't my grown children talk to me?

What am I avoiding or denying by constantly working?

When was the last time I felt truly at peace?

Whenever the emerging story begins to feel like a burden, or a saga featuring an innocent victim of injustice, it is time to end the conversation and dig into uncomfortable realms beyond the story line. Without excavating, we may only reenact the known portion of our story over and over again, seeing future circumstances as continuations of old themes. Breaking ground, we uncover the limiting beliefs that have been imprisoning us in murkiness.

Digging for Treasure

The accounts that follow trace the struggles of two women who broke through to the limiting beliefs robbing them of happiness. Finding buried treasure, each was able to stop recapitulating her life story and tap into resources teeming with fresh energy.

Plagued by unworthiness. According to Janice, the breakup of her marriage was just a continuation of her life story of abuse, low self-esteem, failure at relationships, and self-blame. "It's all my fault," she said of the divorce. Janice began letting go of her story by healing painful childhood memories of physical and sexual abuse. She then examined messages she'd received about being unlovable and found ways to nurture all parts of herself. Soon after she'd started rollerblading and losing weight, I asked her to evaluate where in her life she still felt challenged.

During her next session she said, "I am challenged in my relationships. I don't know how to ask for what I want. I want each relationship to be an equal give-and-take, but I'm still the one making the phone calls when I want to get together with friends. I'd like *them* to occasionally call *me*."

"What comes up inside when you think about asking for something you want?" I asked.

"That I won't get it, so why ask," she replied anxiously.

"And why won't you get it?"

"Because I don't deserve to get what I want." Her eyes filled with tears. "Even though I'm having fun and doing important things for myself, a part of me still thinks it's undeserving. No amount of feeling good seems to help that part feel worthy."

"It's great that you have this awareness," I said. "And I would like to suggest that feeling *bad* is not about worthiness either. Feeling good or bad really doesn't affect the part that feels unworthy. I wonder what does?"

She paused. "I don't know. Somehow I just need to *get it.*"

"Yes, somehow we just have to *get* that we are worthy. Our worthiness as human beings is not based on our performance, behavior, social circumstances, or financial status. Nor does it come from feeling loved or valued as a child."

Janice could not break free of her story because she held a limiting belief that kept it going: she believed she was not worthy enough to ask for what she wanted. She had never paused to consider that she might have formulated this belief herself. Together we examined a compelling proposition: What if worthiness is a gift that comes wrapped in the package called birth? In this case, our first breath would provide evidence that we are worthy. In other words, what if we are worthy *just because we were born?*

Many of us, like Janice, do not harbor this awareness. In fact, we grew up believing all messages to the contrary. We *chose* to believe those messages about our worth because we knew of no others. And we used this input as evidence that we are *not* worthy of love or happiness, that we are *not* to be valued.

Most of these messages, spoken and unspoken, came in early childhood, when beliefs are readily seeded. Shamed for our behavior, we internalized the shaming and grew up believing we were bad. Frequently abused—physically, mentally, emotionally, or sexually—we believed the perpetrator's devaluations of us and lost the ability to value ourselves. Constantly put down for our feelings and told to keep quiet, we learned to disrespect our emotions and our talent for self-expression. But none of these internalized messages states a truth about who we are. In effect, deep-seated unworthiness is rooted in a lifetime spent believing lies.

Janice's belief about her unworthiness, based on her internalized childhood experiences, kept her from having a healthy intimate relationship. She was comfortable giving love and attention, but not receiving it. Doubt was always in her mind: *Does he really love me?*

Is he showing me he cares, or is he just being nice until the one he truly wants comes along? Eventually Janice was willing to change her limiting belief and reunite with her inherent worthiness.

Embracing this treasure, she let her story go and her worldview shifted. No longer did she need friends and lovers to affirm her innate value. The knot of anxiety that she had long felt in the pit of her stomach, vanished. She began to feel at home in the world. Shortly after, she met a man who mirrored her newfound worthiness and continually encouraged her to share her genuine feelings.

Haunted by fear. Mary was trying desperately to control her destructive impulses to rage, shame, and blame. She grew up in a small midwestern town with a raging mother, and was forever fending off her verbal and physical attacks. Fear was Mary's constant companion. She had no safe place to go.

Her story featured persecution, betrayal, fear, and a need to protect herself by destroying her oppressor. As a forty-year-old mother of two, she knew she was once again enacting the script. Horrified by her raging behavior, which erupted unpredictably and spewed forth onto her children and husband, Mary feared she would and could ruin everything in her world. She often dreamt that her neighborhood was a wasteland of shattered houses and charred earth, causing her to feel homeless and lost.

Mary began working through her theme of betrayal. But she could not shake loose the fear that in facing her oppressor she herself might be destroyed. This limiting belief was enshrined beyond her story line, and to work through it she had to see that blaming her misery and anger on external circumstances only gave rise to more feelings of persecution and exposure. Digging courageously into unexplored parts of herself, she found the real threat to her safety: she had internalized her raging mother and was now terrorized from within.

It was sobering for Mary to look in the mirror and acknowledge her rage, shame, and self-blame. Careful not to judge herself a terrible person, she managed to look past these destructive parts to the disappointment, hurt, and fear that had fueled them. Soon she began to nurture herself with compassion, giving herself what she had long given others who were "acting out" deep pain through destructive behavior.

Self-forgiveness opened the door to Mary's heart. Then self-loving broke through the darkness like rays of sunlight, transforming the raging, wounded part of her. By the time a sense of inner peace and safety had taken the place of Mary's fear and desperate need for protection, the destructive part no longer roamed her inner landscape. Now when her children's behavior aroused anger or frustration, she opened her heart to them and lovingly conveyed her concerns. Responsive loving had replaced reactive raging as her primary mode of communication.

Trapped in the Story

Peering beneath the headlines of our story, we arrive at rich excavation sites. Each one invites us to step out of the story and dig. More than likely, we find a limiting belief that has curbed our growth. Uprooting it, we let go of our story and gain a fresh experience of who we really are.

However, peering beneath the headlines sometimes feels like a waste of time. Life is too crazy, we have too many responsibilities, our to-do list is too long. We think that if we can stay busy and focused, we will be happy. But this did not prove true for Helen.

Helen, in her early fifties, was married and the mother of two grown daughters. She believed that people considered her stupid, inept, and undependable; she expected everyone she knew to abandon her. Indeed, her family treated her this way, and her employer expressed similar sentiments from time to time. Her whole life seemed to be saying, *You are not enough.*

Helen also had trouble completing things. She had begun earning an art therapy degree but stopped just a few credit hours short. An interior designer, she never took the state exam allowing her to practice. She had also started writing a book and wanted to pursue a career as a painter. Just listening to Helen's exploits left me dazed.

"I want to be good at something," she often said. Hearing these words, I suspected that if Helen examined her story she would uncover a limiting belief that she wasn't competent enough and would go on to experience a deep sense of accomplishment. But she couldn't bring herself to do it; her past was too painful and confusing to revisit. Her purpose in coming to me was to learn how to complete more tasks so she could have time to follow her passion. She would begin each appointment by complaining about how little she had accomplished the previous week. Making lists and attending classes in time management gave her more hours, but she felt defeated.

When I asked what would bring her fulfillment and peace, she said she didn't know. Her "doing" was who she thought she was. But since she seemed unable to do enough, she felt she wasn't good enough.

We all know what it is like to be in a rut. It has the familiar ring of *I have been here before. I'm forever feeling overwhelmed, dissatisfied, disappointed, and hurt. I can't do anything right. I'm afraid I will fail. Nothing will ever change for me. It's the story of my life.*

Unexamined life stories are like that. Their tracks are so worn that we go unconscious in them, replaying our habitual thinking and feeling responses. Our every endeavor feels boring, repetitive, and numbing. Despair and futility follow.

Contrast this ordeal with the experience of examining life stories, uncovering limiting beliefs, and letting go of the stories. Figure 5–1, on page 51, shows some common distinctions.

Perhaps you are stuck in your story and ready to move on. If so, prepare for major changes. For one thing, when you slide out of your customary scenario, your mood will lift. All that was deadening before may now be life affirming. For another, your perspective will shift: instead of life happening to you, or even pummeling you, you will be *creating* it. With the eradication of limiting beliefs comes a leap from glimpsing new options to implementing them.

It is also true that excavating for limiting beliefs can be labor intensive. So from time to time step back from your investigations,

Figure 5–1

STAYING STUCK	LETTING GO
Boring	Fresh
Tired	Energized
"Something isn't right."	"All is well."
Despair/Depression	Creativity/Enthusiasm
Overwhelm	Balance
Apathy	Wonder and awe
Controlled	Spontaneous
Contracted	Expanded

take a deep breath, and soften your focus. You just might glimpse a new possibility.

Throughout, exercise patience and compassion. Remember that once upon a time you were a young, vulnerable child. Every belief you chose to call your own was the best option available to you. Now, however, "once upon a time" is over and your choices are endless.

CHAPTER SIX

BLACK-AND-WHITE THINKING

You say tomato, and I say tomahto.
You say potato, and I say potahto.
Tomato, tomahto
Potato, potahto
Let's call the whole thing off.

These are the lyrics of a tune I sang growing up. Most young children at the time were happier singing than bickering over pronunciations. Black-and-white thinking—right-and-wrong, good-and-bad, appropriate-and-inappropriate, moral-and-immoral polarizations—meant little to us. This limitation of the mind had not yet made its dent. But soon enough, it did.

The Importance of Being Right

Being right is very important in our culture. People who correctly answer the teacher's questions go to the front of the class. People who know what they're doing get ahead in everything they tackle. For all intents and purposes, their lives look happy, prosperous, and in control. In fact, because they know all the right answers and have things so well figured out, these are considered the *right people*—to know, to talk about, to model ourselves after.

On the other hand, the wrong answers get us in trouble. We can be punished, or left out. The wrong approach shows a basic lack of intelligence, common sense, upbringing, and good taste.

Being right is so important we ardently defend it. The subtext goes something like this: "If you don't see things the way I do, isn't one of us wrong and other right? If I argue with you, one of us is incorrect, correct? And I argue with you *because* you are off base and need to be set right, if only for the record. Come to think of it, my way of thinking is right, so I will show it to you. And yes, I do believe my thoughts because they are right!"

These statements are loaded with limiting beliefs and self-judgments. To see how limiting our beliefs are when we know we are right, reflect on the following situations:

- You had the right answer and things didn't work out as planned.

- You implemented the right approach at work and were accused of being inconsiderate and overbearing.

- You did everything right in your relationship and still your partner fell in love with someone else.

- You needed more time to do a project right, and by then it was too late.

- You said all the right things—you made your point, held your position, enumerated why this course would work—and no one wanted to talk to you.

The self-judgments that come with right-and-wrong thinking are scathing. Here are some examples:

- *I'm so ashamed of messing up that I don't want anyone to find out.*

- *I lost the love of my life because I totally blew it.*

- *Nothing I do works out; I'm treated unfairly. I'm just a loser.*

- *I keep myself in line because I'm terrorized by making mistakes.*

Being right doesn't always get you what you want, nor does it help you feel good about yourself. The same holds true for being good, appropriate, or moral. Black-and-white thinking in all its manifestations spells trouble. This narrowly focused, punitive way of seeing ourselves limits our experience of who we are.

The Pitfall of Black-and-White Thinking

George was raised by a father who considered himself right and everyone else was wrong. Pleasing Father became the unspoken family code, and not knowing the right answer or the proper way to behave brought dire consequences. Just the thought of having to face his father struck fear in George's heart.

George realized early on that his father was usually right, which meant that George and his siblings were wrong—a lot. Being wrong and being told he was wrong felt awful, so George decided at a young age to stop caring about being wrong or right. The place inside that hurt each time he was judged for being wrong had simply shut down, and little by little it died. When I met George at age forty-one, his biggest fear was that he would "become" his father. And he had all the right reasons for thinking it would be the most terrible fate possible.

Unwittingly, George had slipped into the pit of black-and-white thinking. Any behavior that reminded him of his father was wrong and had to be obliterated, stamped out, cut off, and thrown away. I, too, was deemed dangerously out of line for suggesting that seeing his father as the problem kept George entrenched in pain and emotional numbness. George expended vital energy making sure he was different from father. In response, his stress levels soared. He could not sleep at night. His kidneys ached constantly. He kept losing his temper at work. And the more he obsessed, the more his behavior mirrored his father's.

George was caught in a web of his own making, trapped in a limited view of himself based on the "goodness" or "badness" of his behavior. While acting unlike his father, he considered himself good; while acting like his father, he saw himself as bad. And one afternoon he saw himself as very bad.

On that day George and I were able to explore what happened inside him when he behaved like his father. He explained that he felt blamed and shamed—exactly what he had experienced as a young boy. Judged by his father as a child, he was judging himself now as an adult. His judgment was causing stress, self-loathing, and self-recrimination, keeping the numb, shut-down part inside frozen.

Recognizing that he had in fact become the tyrannical black-and-white thinker he had judged within himself, George began to climb out of the pit of pain and numbness. His first sure steps came the moment he took responsibility for behaving precisely like his father, an action known in the healing arts as "owning the projection." Movement in his black-and-white thinking about his father's behavior followed as the frozen place inside him began to thaw. That frozen place was his heart.

Engaging the Heart

The heart—the energetic center of compassion, loving, acceptance, and forgiveness of ourselves and others—shuts down when we adopt black-and-white thinking. This form of thinking is a measure we resort to out of a desperate need to stay in control of our lives and make sense of the world. At such times, great stores of energy are required to reject what we see as wrong (bad, inappropriate, immoral) and cling to what we see as right (good, appropriate, moral). When the heart opens, making sense of the world is not as important as being happy, finding peace, feeling healthy and stress free, and getting a good night's sleep. Pursuing these missions, we allow our heart to thaw around the frozen hurts and fears, and gradually free ourselves from the grip of control. We then begin to live authentically.

Engaging the heart is always an option. If you, like George, have slipped into the pit of black-and-white thinking, consider these heart openers. First, while self-*right*eously judging others, look at your own behavior. Then ask yourself these questions:

✧ Do I judge a part of *me* in the same way?

✧ Am I judging others' mistakes because *I* am afraid of failing?

✧ Do I judge anger as wrong (bad, inappropriate, immoral) in others because I see it as wrong in *myself?*

✧ Do certain people get on my nerves because I'm afraid their behavior resembles *my own?*

Second, if it turns out that you really are criticizing others while secretly judging yourself, admit to the projection and take responsibility for it. Also expect resistance. Our inner controller would much rather feel right than look at its imperfections. Besides, finding fault with others keeps things tidy inside and helps us make sense of life. Owning our projections is a giant step forward, though messy because we end up feeling the pain of our judgments.

Third, consider for a moment that this world was designed not to make sense but to foster growth. Imagine your every experience in life as a lesson nudging you to wake up and explore your potential. Following this shift in perception, your heart may open so wide that you will actually feel it thawing.

Following the thaw, anything is possible, including the unthinkable. George, for example, felt a rush of compassion for his father and forgave him. More importantly, he forgave himself, learned the art of patience, let go of shame and blame, and began to treat himself with kindness and love. When he released the punisher within, which had so harshly condemned him and others, his heart began to "speak up" in every segment of his life.

The heart's compassion, forgiveness, patience, self-acceptance, and loving-kindness infuse the mind with a palette of colors far more versatile than black and white. The mind, at last liberated from its two-toned starkness, can hold all sorts of oppositions, transforming them into subtler hues. Together, heart and mind outshine the internalized self-punisher and give birth to a new awareness. We then realize that magnificence, which has nothing to do with to being right, is inherent in our divine nature.

CHAPTER SEVEN

MIND CHATTER

Have you ever noticed an internal monologue running nonstop in the background of your day? Does it wake you at night hashing over a project at work, an unfinished conversation with a friend, a list of your latest worries and "what ifs," or concern for your child or partner? This chatter is a product of the "monkey mind," begging for your attention.

The Monkey Mind

The chattering monkey mind is my companion in the shower every morning. When I tune in, I am amazed at what my mind is saying. Somehow it has taken past events, however incidental, and spun intricate fantasies around them, dramatizing the major players and unfurling potential outcomes. The scenarios are almost always punctuated with negativity. Worse, they elaborate on my greatest fears—of failure, of being judged or excluded, of having unreliable perceptions, and of people talking about me behind my back. As if that were not enough, in the two minutes it takes me to brush my teeth my mind can conjure up three more scenes that have nothing to do with the day's agenda.

By the time I have completed my morning routine, I'm distracted. The day ahead looks awful. I'm so stressed that when my husband greets me with a kiss, I give him little more than a grunt of recognition.

While under the spell of the monkey mind, we are lost in a sort of waking dream. This open-eyed dream state appears so surreptitiously that we often fail to notice it. Having no idea what is going on in the gray matter behind our eyes, we remain mesmerized for hours.

I'll be driving along a busy thoroughfare, courteously minding my own business, when a sports car cuts me off. I spend the next half hour ranting and raving about ill-mannered drivers. Then I pull into a grocery store parking lot, innocently thinking about food for dinner, and another driver steals the space I'm cruising into. At this point I declare war on the next person I see, which turns out to be a young man happily stacking apples in the produce section. I am not a pretty sight.

The chatter of our waking dreams grabs our attention and redirects our behavior. Meanwhile, it spews forth a never-ending monologue about the unfairness of life, our bad luck, and all the people who are out to get us. Although the performance is replete with material for expanding our self-awareness, waking up from it is a challenge.

Held Hostage by Mind Chatter

Teresa had such a challenge. Mother of two young children, she had recently been divorced after fifteen years of marriage. Her ex-husband had agreed to provide for her and the children so she could take two years to establish herself in a new career. Teresa was at peace with the divorce and planned to enroll in acupuncture school, hoping someday to start a practice. But she couldn't bring herself to sign up for classes. So we began to explore possible reasons for her refusal to take the reins of her life.

"Why do I have to do all this inner work?" she complained.

"Why do I have to look at my issues? I just want to live my life and be happy."

"Well, are you happy?" I asked.

"No, I can't seem to budge," she said. Suspecting Teresa was being held hostage by her mind, I asked her to observe her waking dreams over the coming week.

At her next session, she said all the chatter was sabotaging her efforts to create a new life. It had her doubting herself so much, she felt defeated before she could begin. Frustrated, she had withdrawn from friends and stepped out only to shop for food and drive the children to and from school. She wished her mind would leave her alone and wondered why it kept hassling her.

Creating new opportunities while listening to negative mind-chatter is like having one foot on the gas and the other on the brake. So it was no wonder that after months of moving forward in fits and starts, Teresa became exasperated. I suggested she let go of her "why" questions and instead ask herself *what* her mind was telling her and *how* she might engage its support.

On her return visit, Teresa said she'd been paying closer attention to the chatter. Most messages contained serious misgivings about her ability to succeed in business, and in school as well. But she had no idea how to win the support of her monkey mind.

To help her grapple with these limiting perceptions of doubt, I suggested applying the "whats" and "hows" to the bigger picture of her life. In response, she decided to ask herself these questions:

What does it mean to live my life well? What would it look like? What activities and qualities would it encompass?

What makes me happy? What circumstances and experiences contribute to this feeling? How might I integrate more of them into my life?

What can I do inwardly to go through this change with ease? How can I find real support?

While addressing the questions, Teresa plunged into a realm beyond negative mind chatter, identifying many more "whats" and "hows" related to the new reality she envisioned. In the process, she released herself from captivity. No longer held hostage by her mind, she began using it to create possibilities and further expand her awareness. As inertia gave way to forward momentum, she felt increasingly self-confident and soon enrolled in classes that could help her operate a successful business.

The Perils of Ignoring Mind Chatter

Energy follows thought. If thought is narrowly focused and self-debasing, energy will constrict as well. When limitations of the mind take over, energy levels plummet, causing many people to withdraw a bit from friends and loved ones. Allowing mind chatter, in all its negativity, to go unchecked may eventually lead to depression.

Ellen was depressed. She had recently gone through a painful breakup with a man she deeply loved. In her more lucid moments, she could hear her mind chattering on about how this romance was just the latest in a string of failed relationships. Hurt by these harsh judgments against her feelings, her capacity to love, and the part of her that wanted this man back at any cost, she refused to pay attention to the monologues and slowly retreated from everyone she knew for fear of further incrimination.

Entangled in a morass of painful memories, she repeatedly went over details of the breakup. She recited a litany of "if onlys"—if only she had behaved differently, if only she had loved him better—condemning herself for her shortcomings. Her mind chatter, getting the best of her, had shut down her heart.

Soon Ellen began meditating and seeking spiritual guidance. Daily practice led her to her "spiritual heart," a place inside that could hold all feelings without judging them, which she described as being of her yet coming from somewhere beyond her. With her spiritual heart open, she could simultaneously experience unconditional love and her feelings of loss and betrayal. These seemingly opposing feeling states soon expanded her understanding of love. Ellen accessed self-love, self-compassion, and forgiveness for the judgments she held against herself, and little by little she wriggled out of the clutches of depression and addictive behavior. "Loving," she observed, "is something far greater than thinking... and so am I."

Taming the Monkey Mind

The rowdy monkey mind, with all of its negative fantasies, can always be tamed. If you observe it, let its intrusive messages into your consciousness, and use them to refocus on the bigger picture of your life, the noise will begin to fade away. Then the moment you know you are more than your limiting thoughts, the monkey mind will fall silent, its mission accomplished.

But if you disregard this pesky creature, you may become enmeshed in its antics. Tangled in snarls of painful self-assessments, you will begin reacting unconsciously to them, undermining your every effort to move forward. Welcome the discomfort, for it can push you all the way to your core, where an untapped part of you is waiting to be discovered. Glimpsing beyond the monkey mind, you will at once expand your awareness and quiet the chattering. In the ensuing hush, you will know the mind is not the source of truth, and you will be less prone to believe everything you think.

Taming the monkey mind does more than eliminate the constant drone of limiting thoughts. It can free up this energy for focusing, clarifying, gaining insights, and expressing creativity. For many people, the intermittent stillness ushers in signals from their inner guide. Some detect whispers of encouragement; others hear an intoxicating call to their true life purpose.

CHAPTER EIGHT

SEEING ONLY LACK

A group of devotees invited a master of meditation to the house of one of them to give them instruction. He told them that they must strive to acquire freedom from strong reactions to the events of daily life, an attitude of habitual reverence, and the regular practice of meditation which he explained in detail. The object was to realize the one divine life pervading all things.

"In the end you must come to this realization not only in the meditation period, but in daily life. The whole process is like filling a sieve with water."

He bowed and left.

The little group saw him off, and then one of them turned to the others, fuming. "That's as good as telling us that we'll never be able to do it. Filling a sieve with water, I ask you! That's what happens now, isn't it? At least, it does with me. I go to hear a sermon, or I pray, or I read one of the holy books, or I help the neighbors with their children and offer the merit to God, or something like that, and I feel uplifted. My character does improve for a bit—I don't get so impatient, and I don't gossip so much. But it soon drops off, and I'm just like I was before. It is like water in a sieve, he's right there. But now he's telling us this is all we shall ever be able to do."

They pondered on the image of the sieve without getting any solution which satisfied them all. Some thought he was telling them that people like themselves in the world could expect only a temporary upliftment; some thought he was just laughing at them. Some thought he was telling them there was something fundamentally wrong with their ideas. Others thought he might be referring to something in the classics which he had expected them to know; they looked for references to a sieve, without success.

In the end the whole thing dropped away from all of them except one woman, who made up her mind to see the master. He gave her a sieve and a cup, and they went to the nearby seashore, where they stood on a rock with the waves breaking round them.

"Show me how you fill the sieve with water," he said.

She bent down, held the sieve in one hand, and scooped the water into it with the cup. It barely appeared at the bottom of the sieve, and then was gone.

"It's just like that with spiritual practice too," he said, "while one stands on the rock of I-ness, and tries to ladle the divine realization into it. That's not the way to fill the sieve with water, or the self with divine life."

"How do you do it then?" she asked.

He took the sieve from her hand, and threw it far out into the sea, where it floated momentarily and then sank.

"Now it's full of water," he said, "and it will remain so. That's the way to fill it with water, and it's the way to do spiritual practice. It's not ladling little cupfuls of divine life into the individuality, but throwing the individuality far out into the sea of divine life."

—TREVOR LEGGETT[1]

Like the students in Trevor Leggett's story, many of us see ourselves as lacking and yearn for fullness. These perceptions of lack keep us frustratingly busy. We work overtime pouring into ourselves cupful after cupful of one bounty or another, expecting in return some assurance of our goodness, perfection, or belovedness. But rarely does it come. We ration out energy, time, money, and attention, fearful that they may not be replenished. Sure enough, these fears prove true.

Our organs of perceptions are similar to the master's sieve. Looking out at the world from the vantage point of lack, we see insufficiency. There's not enough time in the day, money to go around, food to feed the people, peaceful discussion among adversaries, neighborly tolerance, justice, fairness, or safety.

The inner landscape looks just as bleak. We're not smart, talented, loved, lucky, educated, attractive, or kind enough. The media remind us that to measure up socially we need a high-paying job with benefits, a retirement fund, a mortgage, two children, an SUV, and a well-trained dog. Invariably we come up short, and a subtle but palpable desperation seeps into our lives like a bad taste that won't go away.

Ladling for Goodness

Susan knew as a child that she wanted to be good. Raised Catholic, she decided as a young adult to enter a convent and be of service in the world. She spent years teaching children in gang- and drug-infested neighborhoods of a major metropolitan city. Eventually she left the convent and dedicated herself to assisting her family and community.

At age fifty-nine, she sat in my office discouraged and depressed, her eyes dulled with pain. Although she had spent decades trying to fill her sieve with acts of devotion, each cupful seemed to seep right through her, prompting her to dip in over and over again. Her lifetime of service had not imbued her with a sense of goodness. To the contrary, she felt inept and saw her acts of helpfulness and kindness as substandard. She was sure she had missed her mark in life.

Tracing the roots of Susan's depression to a limiting perception of her inner nature, I suggested she carefully examine the holes she felt inside her. Upon reflection, she said they may have been forged by self-judgments anchored in beliefs she'd adopted as a young child. Very early on, she was taught that goodness is earned through self-denial and sacrificial deeds. She was told to emulate selfless, holy people; compare herself with them; and vow to outperform them. She accepted the mission, and with it the hope that a selfless life would be deeply rewarding. But she never envisioned herself a selfless, holy person, and as time passed she began to feel like an imposter.

Recognizing at last that her childhood beliefs did indeed shape her view of herself, Susan challenged them one by one until her holes began to fill with her true essence. The glimmers of divinity that shone through startled her into the realization that goodness was present within her, inherent in her nature. This discovery expanded her heart, and she realized that the goodness she had been dipping into was actually her own. Eventually her depression lifted and a sparkle returned to her eyes. Smiling, she said, "I feel a desire to return to a life of service. This time, though, I want to assist others out of the fullness inside me."

Striving for Perfection

Mark, a middle-aged husband, father of three, and corporate executive, had just returned from a two-week backpacking trip in the wilderness. It was the first solo expedition he'd taken as a married man, and true to form he had a purpose: to evaluate his priorities. His hectic work schedule had gotten the better of him, so much so that he rarely saw his children anymore. During the few precious hours he had with his wife, he was either too exhausted or distracted to enjoy her company. He had expected more of himself, certain that he could carve out a life of perfection—a well-calibrated balance of loving husband, attentive father, and prosperous, venerated CEO.

The day after his return, he seemed exceptionally invigorated. "The wilderness put me in touch with real abundance, inside and out. Looking around, I saw nothing but majesty and beauty. It's like nature filled me up. I felt so alive out there."

YOU CAN MAKE IT HEAVEN

"And what's it like being back in the city?" I asked.

"So far, so good. But I have no clue how to hold on to that sense of expansiveness while dealing with all the hassles of corporate life. In nature they fade away, but not here. Even after escaping the office, fighting the crosstown traffic, and making it home, I can't unwind, because my wife and children deserve the very best from me. The harder I try to keep up with my life, the more I lose sight of its blessings."

I asked if he felt joy in this straight-jacket kind of existence. He confessed that he didn't, that with all the facades and props in his world he could barely feel *anything*. "But I'm sure I can get it together," he added. "If I play all my cards right, everything will be perfect."

I could almost hear Mark's sieve leaking. To reinvigorate his perceptions of fullness, I asked him to gauge the distance between his lackluster life and the glittery picture-perfect one in his imagination.

At our next session Mark was less animated. He acknowledged that his treadmill reality was miles from his vision of grandeur, but was sure he could reach his goal of flawlessness. Caught in this illusion of perfection, Mark could not see the limitations it had imposed on him. He had been seduced right back into a perception of lack and refused to acknowledge it.

"Well, how can you recapture the expansiveness you experienced in the wilderness?" I asked.

"Right now I don't know what to do about seeing the fullness of my life. There doesn't seem to be any time for that," he said, shrugging in resignation.

Last I heard from Mark, things were not going well. He complained about body aches and pains, seeing too little of his family, a significant weight gain, his tennis swing, and his colleagues' presentation skills. According to his doctor, he also had unsatisfactory cholesterol levels and high blood pressure. The window to fullness that Mark opened in the wilderness was now shut tight.

Immersed in Fullness

Portals to the sea of possibility provide points of entry for anyone choosing to take the leap. Indeed, every year countless individuals shed their conditioned or manufactured beliefs and plunge into this realm of fullness. Business executives walk away from six-figure salaries and high-profile jobs, hitting the road in RVs. Distinguished career women retreat to obscure mountain villages accessible only by four-wheel-drive vehicles and E-mail. Most escape with their families; some set up a home office. Few make it back to administrative meetings and power lunches.

Corporate renegades are eager to describe their crowning achievement: an unimaginably expansive existence. Many will tell you they heard a strange "voice" inside, urging them to flee from traffic, cell phones, and news broadcasts, if only for a while. Then once immersed in their newfound profusion of all-that-is, they stopped striving for starched-to-perfection exteriors and decided to stay. They might even whisper that they are wealthier now than ever before, their hearts filled to overflowing. No longer mired in dashed hopes and unrealized expectations, they feel oddly uplifted.

If you have time for a cup of tea together, they will point out that this briny fullness has surprising characteristics. It engenders tolerance for life's wrinkles, for grumpiness and need for breath freshener. It eradicates any meaning previously ascribed to external approval and symbols of achievement. It also induces a shift from "doing" to "being," showing that doing good *comes from* being good. Suddenly everything feels real, authentic, and of one fabric inside and out.

This transformation is strikingly illustrated in *The Blue Faience Hippopotamus* by Joan Grant, a children's book about a huge hippopotamus who falls in love with an elegant princess. Yearning to be near her and win her love, he convinces a magician to turn him into a blue ceramic hippo that she can purchase. His wish comes true, and the princess takes great delight in the exquisite little hippo, carrying him with her everywhere. But after a while a different trinket captures her attention, and she leaves the hippo on her dressing table amidst other discarded objects of her affection.

Although rejected, the hippo retains his great love for the princess and turns his final wish over to her. The magician, moved by the hippo's desire to give of himself completely, transforms him into a human infant—something the princess could indeed love forever.

You too can love yourself into realness and fulfillment. The first step is to recognize any conclusions you have drawn about being "less than" your picture of perfection. As you release them, the truth of your being will bathe your senses and your heart will open wide. No longer will feelings of inadequacy mar your vision. Like the born-again VIPs and the at last euphoric hippo, you will see fullness everywhere.

CHAPTER NINE

THE MASKS OF FEAR

A few years ago while backpacking with friends, I agreed to tag along as far as I could to the top of a nearby peak. Holding back my fear of edges, I made it halfway up the slope, then I spotted the rim and my legs turned to mush. Collapsing, I clung to a rock and froze in a fetal position until a friend, prying me loose, assisted me down the mountain. There I burst into tears, grateful to be safe at last.

Embarrassment followed, and I began reprimanding myself. *This is irrational,* I snarled. *As I child I was fearless, but now I'm terrified of plummeting into canyons. When did I become such a wimp? Why couldn't I just enjoy the hike like everyone else?*

For days I seethed with anger, berating myself for a crescendo of shortcomings: foolishness for having a fear of edges, weakness for letting it incapacitate me, incompetence for needing a friend to walk me down the slope. *You're a first-class loser,* my monkey mind proclaimed every so often, with increased intensity. The shame and blame kept me out of the woods and off the trails I loved.

The Urge to Conceal Fear

Fear, a normal human response to a perceived danger, is not always sanctioned by our culture. It is okay to scream in terror while watching a horror film but unacceptable to fear failure. The fear of failure is deemed a sign of weakness. It is fine to fear the dark, but taboo to fear being unloved. This fear is said to denote a character flaw. Also unsanctioned are fears of being alone, of loss, getting hurt, insolvency, rejection, betrayal, abandonment, aging, dying, and countless others. When we are in the grip of any fear considered inappropriate, our impulse is to save face by masking it.

The masks of fear come in a variety of shapes. Those most commonly used are anger, control, and obsessive behavior. But while such cover-ups may hide a fear from the outside world, they cannot diminish the fear, nor can they alleviate the judgments that were internalized along with it. When this self-condemnation becomes so painful that we do not feel safe enough inside to face our fears, we deny their existence.

The Drama of Denial

Joan, a fifty-year-old bank teller, occasionally alluded to an early history of traumatic events but refused to discuss them. It was apparent that her body still harbored her childhood fears, for she would react intensely at the mention of sensitive issues. In general, she went to great lengths to preserve her facade of denial.

Because Joan was so defended against her fears, one drama after another began running her life. If she was not fighting with her boss, she was upset about a neighbor's runaway cat. Her car was forever on the brink of breaking down, as was one appliance after another in her small apartment. These theatrics kept her riveted on outer events, miles away from her inner tumult. But at night she would wake with body aches and pains; worries kept her churning for hours, robbing her of much needed rest and the capacity to deal with stress.

To keep her fears out of view and self-reproach at bay, Joan sought to control everything and everyone in her world—her physical aches and pains, others' opinions, her boss's moods, her landlord's expectations, and her friends' schedules. She would arrive at her sessions fuming with resentment at the demands placed on her the previous week. She criticized each one, reserving her harshest judgments for the pain she felt between her shoulder blades, her feelings of overwhelm, and her inability to cope with life. She had lost all compassion for herself.

It was time for Joan to turn on the bright lights, to see a truer picture of her essence. But her judgments so clouded her view of herself, she refused. When I gently suggested we dig beneath the need to control her universe, she said, "Oh, what's the use. Nothing will ever change." When I recommended looking at her self-criticism, in the hope of relieving her aches and pains, she blamed them on outside circumstances. When I asked what she was afraid of, her eyes glazed over with panic. Like a deer caught in the headlights of an oncoming vehicle, she froze, too anxious to face her fears.

To numb the anxiety, Joan began overeating. This new mask made it even more difficult for her to access her fears and the self-condemnation they had spawned. So tenacious was her denial of fear that during our sessions she could barely speak. Her defenses had zapped her of all vitality.

Symptoms of Denial

Each new mask of fear further limits us, compounding our challenge to lead a sane, healthy life. Fortunately, outward symptoms of denial can alert us to impending damage. To find out whether you might be in denial about an underlying fear, explore these questions:

✣ **Do you rise quickly to anger over trivialities?** Fanning the flames of anger is a clever diversion for anyone wishing to avert an encounter with fear. It warms the body, jangles the nerves, and keeps a steady stream of blood coursing palpably through the veins, drowning out deeper feelings.

❧ *Do you attempt to control outer events, unsightly behavior, the flow of conversation, and the time you spend with others?* Imposing regulations on day-to-day routines evokes a temporary sense of power over fear. Redirecting social discourse, changing the subject, and avoiding awkward situations preserves a semblance of safety.

❧ *Have you noticed any obsessive behavior patterns?* Overeating, overdrinking, overspending, and other excessive preoccupations temporarily quiet the nervous energy of anxiety. The mind, numbed, is less apt to drift off for a rendezvous with fear.

Disturbing world events can trigger a similar response, most often obsessive overextension. Does your stomach churn at the thought of diminished safety and security? Are you dragging yourself from task to task, bone tired but never settling down long enough to relax? Is your inner taskmaster telling you, *Keep moving, or desperation is sure to creep steadily higher on the radar screen?*

This on-the-go, can't-stop, don't-have-time pattern of behavior fools us into believing we can outrun fear until we collapse in bed at night oblivious to it. Sleep, however, rarely stops the merry-go-round for more than a few hours. Many people resort to medication to keep their heads from spinning, but end up even more distanced from their fears and questioning their sanity. The only way to reverse these debilitating effects of denial is to confront the fear itself.

Unmasking Fear

Prying off the masks of fear is sometimes scary yet always rewarding. For me, many baby steps were required to lift the anger covering my fear of edges. First, I had to unwind enough to consider returning to a mountain trail. This I did by separating the voice of condemnation from the fear. When the two were at last disentangled, I saw that the judgments, and not the fear, had kept me in the valley.

Next, I decided to tackle a trail while forming an inner zone of refuge and protection. Climbing the slope, I comforted the part of me that was mortified of edges, offering it kindness and compassion. I still felt fear, but I accepted its presence without wondering *why* it was my constant escort. I told it, *We are all right. You're afraid, but that's okay too.* With repeated excursions, I began to feel safer.

During a recent edge experience, I managed to let go of fear for a few moments—just long enough to be swept up in a serenity that seemed to reflect the gently sloping piñon-studded vistas stretching clear to the horizon. I marveled at nature's beauty and harmony, and at the newfound peace permeating the core of my being. As fear returned, I embraced it along with this peace. Both were present, and equally accepted.

Now my day hikes along rims are free of both anger and its twin progeny—blame and shame. I've never figured out the reason for this fear of edges, but I have unlocked a greater truth: fear is my friend. Rather than condemn it, I treat it gently and lovingly. In return, it brings gifts of safety and trust. These I add to the awareness, strength, and empowerment it has already awakened within me.

Lest you think that loving an unmasked fear might only indulge it and reactivate it, I can assure you that quite the opposite is true. While loving your fear, you can walk with it; while judging it you cannot, for self-reproach only incapacitates us. Loving your fear and taking baby steps forward may even diminish it. As the cowardly lion in *The Wizard of Oz* demonstrates, when we embrace our fear, anything is possible.

CHAPTER TEN

THE "FOILED AGAIN" PLAYING FIELD

Self-limitations confine us to a narrow playing field. Limiting beliefs keep us stuck in our life story; limiting thoughts trap us in black-and-white thinking and in mind chatter; limiting perceptions bind us to impressions of scarcity and lack; limiting judgments stop us from befriending our fears. Like the Magic Eye image on page 2, new vantage points reveal a bigger truth, but only for a moment. Very soon we return to the dots on the page, foiled in our efforts to break free of them once and for all.

On this Foiled Again playing field we experience the human condition. Many balk at its frustrations, routines, or garden-variety atmosphere, and wish to evacuate. *Please*, we implore, *let me be special. Let me stand out from the crowd, be different from everyone I know.* But judging human nature only narrows our view of humanity.

Actually, human nature is our teacher. It shows us where we are stuck, how we limit ourselves, where we are unhealed, what we refuse to take responsibility for, and who we would rather blame instead. The only sure deliverance is through expansion into our divine nature, which takes place on a bigger playing field. To get there we must first learn our lessons on the Foiled Again field, study its game plan, then consciously choose to move on.

The Game Plan

Although various games are played on the Foiled Again field, they all adhere to a single game plan best illustrated by the Looney Tunes characters known as Wile E. Coyote and Road Runner. Wile E. Coyote tries perpetually to catch Road Runner. He sets traps, devises clever strategies, and takes great pains to outsmart and outmaneuver the bird, but he does not succeed. Road Runner is always just out of reach.

In this game plan, motives are of secondary importance. Wile E. Coyote's motives are not even clear. He might be hungry, or itching to compete and overpower, or acting purely out of instinct. Maybe he is stuck in his story of a never-ending chase. Road Runner, on the other hand, is intent on minding his own business and goes happily about his days, dashing along the road. Whenever he meets up with one of Wile E. Coyote's pranks, he becomes suddenly circumspect.

What matters most is the curious outcome. Each cartoon in the series builds to a climax with Wile E. Coyote thinking he finally has Road Runner. He's succeeded; he's reached his goal; he's in the right place at the right time; he got away with his scheme; he outwitted his opponent. But his triumph is short-lived, because sure enough, life foils his plan. Similarly, Road Runner's hope for a care-free romp is thwarted.

These characters portray different aspects of human nature. Wile E. Coyote symbolizes the part of us that wants to compete and conquer—that expects success, regardless of the cost, when we have completed our mission. Road Runner represents the part that thinks life happens to us, that our days would be hassle free if only others would leave us alone, that we must be wary because they're out to get us. In both instances, disillusionment strikes repeatedly but the characters recommit to the effort, determined to "do it right" the next time.

The Foiled Again game plan requires players to compete and attempt to make their mark by vanquishing the opponent. The opponent can be an obvious rival or it can be a marital partner, a coworker, a personal attribute that we judge, or life itself. In all instances, the game plan has each contestant vying to outrank the other. But alas, there are no victories—only constant replays.

Of the dozens of games played on this field, here are the top ten, along with perceptions that give rise to them:

PERCEPTION	GAME
1. Win versus lose	Let's Get Even
2. Superior versus inferior	I'm Better Than You
3. Too much versus not enough	There's Never Enough
4. Right versus wrong	I'm Correct; You're Mistaken
5. Good versus bad	Am I Okay?
6. Fair versus unfair	I Want Justice
7. Perpetrator versus victim	You're Out to Get Me
8. Connection versus separation	I Don't Need Anyone
9. Overresponsibility versus blame	Poor Me
10. Loyalty versus abandonment	I Can't Trust You

Fortunately, more satisfying games exist, but they take place in that larger arena, the Self-Mastery playing field. Here the game plan is radically different. Players are required to engage their divine nature in addition to their human nature. Also, there are no opponents—only awareness, growth, and cocreation. Nor are there losers; all outcomes are win-win. Best of all, there is no chance of falling into a rut and repeating the same counterproductive moves over and over again. You get as many turns as it takes to succeed, each producing a new result. And success is measured not by stopwatches, trophies, and certificates, but by the truths that begin to show up inside you. Before stepping onto this new playing field, however, you must give up the old games.

Giving Up an Old Game

Let's Get Even, the most popular game played on the Foiled Again field, had kept Meg engrossed for quite some time, though she did not know it. Divorced after a fifteen-year marriage, Meg knew only that she had finally managed to replace her raging inner critic with an innocent, newly discovered part of her that required nurturing and protection. For months she had not unleashed a tirade of punitive self-judgments. No longer was she imprisoned in a torture chamber of self-hatred and self-doubt. But Meg still could not move forward.

Although she had dreamt what it would feel like to be supported in creating a life of unbridled joy, she had no idea how to get there, or how to be loyal to an inner truth. It soon became clear that mind chatter was bogging her down in feelings of unfairness, hurt, and resentment about her divorce. Some part of her wanted to even the score and show the world how much she counted.

Meg was astounded to discover how immersed she was in the Let's Get Even game. It turned out she'd been playing it since early in her marriage and had learned the game plan so well it had become second nature to her (see figure 10–1). Realizing that this game is what had stymied her, she resolved to quit playing and move on to the field that invited an ongoing relationship with her divine nature. Here, Meg knew, she'd be liberated at last from her win-lose headlock and free to be true to herself.

Telltale Signs That It's Time to Quit

Foiled Again games drive us to such oblivion that you may not realize you are in uniform once again and heading for center field, eager for the shiny plaque. But before reengaging in another game destined for defeat, look inside for pain, discontentment, mild anxiety, or lack of purpose. Scan the horizon for a two-by-four

Figure 10–1

MEG'S "LET'S GET EVEN" GAME AT A GLANCE

Limiting judgments about feelings
1. I am deeply hurt about my marriage ending. I'm a loser for feeling hurt.
2. I was treated unfairly, and my feelings never mattered.
3. Feelings are overwhelming and must be avoided.

Limiting perceptions
1. I have made a mess of my life.
2. I am not smart or talented enough.
3. I cannot survive outside of that marriage.

Limiting beliefs
1. I lost fifteen years to the marriage.
2. I deserve to get what I want out of life. That will even the score.
3. If I don't look out for myself, who will?
4. I must make sure this never happens again.

Underlying fears
1. Of abandonment
2. Of poverty
3. Of rejection
4. Of failure

---

pummeling you into wakefulness. Sniff about for recurring events, or for old damaging thoughts or feelings appearing in this new context, and for recurring events. If any of these telltale signs of game playing captures your attention, stop in your tracks and trace your outer circumstances to the inner state they reflect. Then name the game and turn in your resignation.

Perhaps your boss expects you to work overtime, sacrificing your allegiance to family or personal interests. If so, your boss is most likely mirroring a part of you that is just as demanding, shaming you into submission against your innermost wishes. You might be playing the You're Out to Get Me game, or Poor Me. Chances are you're a star player, a veteran of many years. Your next move, then, is to give notice—not to your boss, but to yourself—and establish more self-nurturing ground rules.

Or perhaps you have been overspending, compulsively draining your credit card accounts to beautify your life. Now, as you attempt to wade through the financial crisis, collection agencies are hounding you daily and your billing privileges are about to be revoked. Your life is anything but beautiful. Consider this a wake-up call to name your game—it could be the There's Never Enough game, or Am I Okay? or even I'm Better Than You—and disengage.

Quitting a game that has for years been shaping your behavior is no small challenge. It takes courage and fortitude to terminate these long-standing contracts we have with our limiting perceptions, renounce our familiar forms of identification, and step forward to greet the unknown. Excitement bubbles up over the prospect of more promising outcomes, yet its edges are tainted with trepidation. Your monkey mind will tell you why it won't work to give up the game: *What will the neighbors think? How will you win the support of family and friends?* Your inner controller will attempt to intimidate you with warnings about countless discomforts. Like the sirens luring Odysseus to shore, these voices will do everything possible to seduce you back into the game.

Any time you feel your resolve weakening, you can always fortify it. For starters, you can review the past season's record. After so many fumbled attempts to get your life together, did you secure that brass ring or did you self-medicate in the wake of each new defeat? In addition, you can refocus on the picture you may have seen of a more promising mission. When you are finally determined to bail out of the old game, give yourself a congratulatory pat on the back and hurry along, because your true self is waiting.

PRACTICE

LEAVING THE "FOILED AGAIN" PLAYING FIELD

When you are fed up with Foiled Again game results, there is no need to keep playing and good cause for quitting. Say good-bye to the old field by following these four steps.

❧ Identify the top two or three games you play.

❧ For each game, write down the limitations you have encountered. Ask yourself:

1. What judgments about myself or others support my participation in this game?

2. How do I perceive myself and my world as a result of playing this game?

3. What beliefs does my game playing encourage?

4. If I let go of this game, what fears might arise?

❧ Jot down glimpses you've had of a bigger playing field.

❧ Choose to step onto this larger field. Here you will be welcomed by your new coach: your inner guide.

The breezes at dawn
Have secrets to tell you,
Don't go back to sleep,
You must ask for what you truly want,
Don't go back to sleep.
People are going back and forth across the doorsill
Where two worlds touch,
The door is round and open,
Don't go back to sleep.

—RUMI[2]

PART III

Liberation

*Every step into the vastness of your true nature
releases an old way of seeing.*

TAKING LIFE LESS PERSONALLY

Do you remember the first time you saw photographs of the earth beamed in from outer space? As you gazed at this blue-green planet shimmering like a beautiful ornament in the vastness of the universe, did your world suddenly shrink and your day-to-day turmoils shrivel into insignificance? Many of us viewing our first images of the earth from interstellar space are jolted into a new perception of ourselves: *The universe doesn't revolve around me at all. I am just a minuscule part of it, and there's so much I haven't yet seen.* Against this cosmic backdrop, never again does our life look quite the same.

A similar shift occurs when we expand our awareness inwardly. Inner space, like outer space, is endless, and the farther in we tread, the more distance we gain from our worries, frustrations, and doubts. Anxiety is no longer overwhelming; disappointment ripples through us instead of stinging; trepidation, rather than rocking our world, is now cushioned by a sense that ultimately all is well.

Feeling "bigger" inside, we begin to realize that others' opinions and our personal dramas are much less important than we had thought, and far too encumbering. So we decide to devote ever-deepening attention to the inner realm instead. Embracing the opportunity to inhabit a place we once caught only glimpses of, we settle in and team up with our divinity.

This is the new playing field, the arena of Self-Mastery. Here we take life less personally. Distanced sufficiently from our pains and hardships, we begin to recognize the illusory perceptions that gave rise to them and, through the techniques described in the following chapters, gradually break free of them. The mind, emotions, and ego respond well to these disciplines, pleased to be put to better use.

The game plan on the Self-Mastery field has nothing to do with competing and everything to do with loving. For just as competing fuels constriction, loving feeds expansion. Treated with openhearted love, even the most self-indicting parts inside give way to healing insights, boundless growth, and palpable abundance—in short, a new life.

In this vast arena, progress is marked by a succession of small insights, each further solidifying the ground of understanding. Perfection does not matter; what counts is the willingness to take life less personally so that your loving can pour forth without resistance no matter what is going on around you. By all accounts, inconceivable changes await. So take a deep breath, fasten your seat belt, and prepare for an odyssey into the limitless universe at the core of your being.

THE NATURE OF LIBERATION

STUDENT: What can you tell me about liberation from my old worldview? Sometimes I see a bigger picture unfolding, but at other times I am too caught up in those little dots on the page. Then everything I encounter seems to be about me.

TEACHER: This is a common stumbling block. Notice the part of you that is halting your progress, for that is where you will need to focus your attention.

STUDENT: Well, I seem to lose perspective most often when my feelings are hurt. It's hard to take these situations less personally.

TEACHER: You can only have hurt feelings if a place inside you has been hurting. See these situations as opportunities to find the hurt and heal it.

STUDENT: If I understand you correctly, I feel hurt because I am holding hurt inside, and that part is responding to new situations. But how do I heal the hurt?

TEACHER: Allow loving to come up at these times. You can access loving through forgiveness, compassion, and understanding. In other words, learn how to love through your hurt.

STUDENT: Oh, so when I feel hurt I can know that more loving is about to enter my life.

TEACHER: Yes, but this will take practice. At first, you must let the hurt be a teacher reminding you to open your heart and bathe the pain with love. In time, your heart will open on its own and pour forth loving.

STUDENT: I like the idea of turning hurt feelings into signals for loving. But I still don't see where liberation comes in. It sounds like I won't really be free of the hurt.

TEACHER: Loving will gradually loosen the contraction around the hurt until you are able to let it go. Right from the start, though, you'll be a loving person instead of a hurting one.

STUDENT: Great, morphing is one of my favorite pastimes. When I'm able to release my hurt, will I see the bigger picture? These days, any time my feelings are hurt, I get so wrapped up in myself I begin to think others are *attacking* me.

TEACHER: You will not only *see* the bigger picture, you'll be *living in* it. Instead of imagining yourself at the receiving end of pain, you'll be receiving and giving life's most precious sweetness. What's more, everyone around you will benefit.

CHAPTER ELEVEN

OPENING THE HEART

The starting point for any enduring change is the heart. This is the place where we first begin to connect with ourselves. When the heart is guarded, the only guidance we can access comes from others' opinions or our own punitive judgments about ourselves. When the heart opens, we learn to respect, value, and listen to the person whose reflection we see in the mirror.

Unfortunately, most people are more used to opening their hearts to others than to themselves. When tragedy strikes in the community, we rush to the scene with an outpouring of sympathy and support. It is as though we were waiting for an opportunity to open our hearts and express our compassion, if only to feel a sense of connection. But rarely do we direct such outpourings to ourselves. The next time you reach out to another, ask yourself: *Am I also reaching out to myself? Am I nurturing the place inside me that needs compassion and love?*

Martha was not. She directed a Big Brother and Big Sister program in a small midwestern town. Everyone in the community praised Martha's big heart and her selfless service to the program. She showered her immediate family, nieces, and nephews with adoration, and had nothing but kindness and compassion for strangers. However, she was living in a silent hell. Through years of counseling she had healed memories and wounds from childhood abuse, and had forgiven her transgressors. But Martha did not love herself.

Trapped in black-and-white thinking, she was devastated any time she fell short of her picture of perfection. She punished herself for a never-ending series of "stupid" actions. She detested her body each time she gained weight. She lashed out at herself whenever shyness held her back from visiting her friends.

Martha's self-hatred finally drove her life into crisis. Her body ached, her health declined, her job posed mounting struggles, her finances flew out of control, and her social life diminished to an occasional phone conversation. The rest of the time she told her friends little lies to cover up her increasingly erratic behavior. Martha was suffering miserably, isolated in a prison of her own making.

When we began to work together, she was aware of her self-punitive tendencies and her feelings of alienation. But Martha did not realize that despite her release of past violations, the judgment-infested part of her was still hurting and was unwilling to be loved.

Any time a part inside is hurting, its pain resonates throughout the inner world, often spilling into the outer one as well. No amount of support or compassion from the outside world can diminish this suffering. On the contrary, such displays of affection are apt to feel threatening to a self-deprecating part that does not want to be loved, arousing unconscious anxieties. To be accepted, the loving must come from within, through opening the heart.

Creating a Safe Place Within

Learning to open the heart and love a part inside that does not want to be loved takes strength and determination. The first step is to create a safe place within, because the voices inside can be scathing. They may rumble with scorn *(You were doing just fine. Why are you changing things?)*, disdain *(If you soften up, you'll look like a fool)*, or outright contempt *(Now I'm sure there's something seriously wrong with you.).* The last thing they want is to have you disturb the status quo, which they believe serves your best interest.

When you are ready to face the chorus, take a deep breath, select an inner space, and declare it a blame-free zone—a place where all parts of you can speak openly without fear of censure or banishment. Then listen as they state their grievances, resentments, or hostility. After hearing and acknowledging those on the front line of self-criticism, you will be able to peel away this layer of judgment. Soon other layers will appear, revealing hurts and deep despair about how unsalvageable you are *(Nothing will ever change. You'll be alone all your life.).* Understand that these convictions were seeded decades ago, when you first denied that you are worthwhile and deserve loving. They too need to be heard and acknowledged with equanimity.

My blame-free zone is an imaginary table—a beautifully crafted yet simple round piece of furniture in the center of a large room. I sit in a comfortable chair at the table, welcoming each grudge, knowing that the alternative is too painful. The first few are usually boisterous, accompanied by threats and accusations; once the fray dies down, quieter and more distressed parts come forth. My job is to hear them all, giving special attention to the despairing ones that were drowned out years ago. If I refrain from challenging these voices, they loosen their grip on me.

Appointing a Compassionate Observer

Once situated in your blame-free zone, appoint a part of you to serve as a compassionate observer that responds to each grudge with acceptance and forgiveness. To fulfill this job description, your compassionate observer must have the capacity to perform these skills:

✿ To listen dispassionately rather than reactively

✿ To pardon all judgments that arise

When I sit at the round table, my compassionate observer is

always present, dispensing acceptance and forgiveness to all manner of grievances and hurt feelings. In response to this loving attention, my heart begins to soften around the edges and gently unfold, revealing a dazzling truth: I am so much more than my anguish.

Such discoveries are possible only because the compassionate observer is detached enough to tackle its assignment and because we gradually identify with this part of us, making its ministrations our own. In giving ourselves over to its acceptance of disabling beliefs, we practice self-acceptance. In directing its acts of forgiveness, we extend self-forgiveness. Both activities are necessary to catalyze an opening of the heart.

Self-acceptance. When we accept a part of ourselves, we admit that it exists. Admitting that I have anger inside is a way of owning this part of me, and in owning it I take responsibility for everything pertaining to it.

For years I didn't. Hearing a nasty comment fly from my lips, I'd ask myself, *How could I have said that? What an awful person I must be.* Feeling anger inside made me think I was especially bad, so I denied its presence. Each time it reared its venomous head, I went numb, oblivious to the destruction it had unleashed within me and the pain it had inflicted on others. Only years later, with my compassionate observer in place, could I accept that I had this feeling inside.

Self-acceptance does not imply agreement with an unwanted feeling, or a decision to act on it. Nor does it assign personal meaning to this feeling, declaring, *You're an abomination for being mad at your mother.* Also, accepting that we have a feeling is not the same as assuming that we *are* that feeling. Self-acceptance simply acknowledges the feeling's presence. Like a bird in a tree, it just *is*—a truth the heart can warm up to.

Every act of self-acceptance frees up our attention, allowing us to explore beneath the surface of an unwanted feeling, acquire rich insights, and gently open our hearts. Imagine for a moment that you are floating along on an ocean of feelings, unwilling to accept that the choppy waves to your left signify anger. If you put on snorkeling gear and dive under them, you will see a whole new world. Beneath the anger, you will most likely find a fear or a hurt.

To gain a sense of the feeling beneath your anger, complete the following sentences:

- ❧ "Each time I think of _____ I feel angry."

- ❧ "When I feel this anger, I am afraid that _____."

- ❧ "When I feel this anger, I am hurt about _____."

Remember, avoid assigning personal meaning to these feelings. Just swim around with your snorkel securely in place, investigating the fear or hurt that lies hidden beneath the anger.

Surfacing briefly, draw conclusions about the role your anger plays. Here are some possibilities:

- ❧ "Anger is a shield protecting a part of me that feels afraid or hurt."

- ❧ "Anger is a red flag alerting me to the presence of a fear or a hurt."

- ❧ "Anger is a messenger informing me that a part inside feels afraid or hurt."

Now take a deep breath and dive again, looking next to the fear or hurt for a judgment it may have spawned, such as the following:

- ❧ "Anyone who knows I'm afraid will reject me."

- ❧ "It's pathetic to be afraid of this."

$\diamond$ "Feeling hurt is a sign of weakness."

$\diamond$ "I'm hurt that they didn't call back. I feel unloved and unworthy of love."

Many people find that anger—whether it serves to protect, alert, or inform—distracts them from the pain of self-judgments. Indeed, the noise, heat, or pure exertion of venting can overpower the most excruciating pangs of self-loathing. It is little wonder that we're so fierce at times!

"Snorkeling" can open the mind to what is really going on in our ocean of feelings. But only self-acceptance can uncover these truths and open the heart.

Self-forgiveness. Forgiving ourselves engages the opening heart, expanding it that much more. Through self-forgiveness we give the hurt parts what they most need—loving pardon for the self-directed judgments they've brought about. In the process, we cease our self-loathing and stop blaming and punishing ourselves. The release of self-imposed judgments is a deeply loving act resulting in a vibrant sense of connectedness and inner peace.

Loving is more than a feeling; it is an action arising from the awakened heart. Stirred from its slumber, the heart sets in motion an awareness of ourselves as loving beings. It is this activity of the heart that gives birth to self-esteem and in turn ignites respect from others.

Betty had lived much of her life dependent on her wealthy parents, even while raising two sons. Emotionally estranged from her highly critical mother, Betty had been in counseling for a year, working on feelings of low self-esteem, shame, blame, and disempowerment. As she started forgiving herself for oppressive judgments about feeling inadequate and permanently flawed, she discovered that she could continue to follow the guidance of her heart and make new choices.

Then one of her sons attempted suicide. Although devastated, Betty was determined to address the crisis. Her newfound capacity for self-forgiveness empowered her to confront her son and resolve past injuries to their relationship.

It also helped her turn around her relationship with her mother. As a young child, Betty longed to express herself openly but refused for fear of her mother's harsh criticism; now she began to come forth from the caring place inside that she had locked away all these years. As Betty shared more of her true self with her mother, she too communicated more endearingly and authentically. No longer hurting, the two giggled on the phone like young schoolgirls.

About this time Betty dreamt that she saved them both from certain death. The loving she had stirred up through self-forgiveness, it seemed, had revitalized the original innocence of her mother-daughter bond and had stopped her internal mother from dying. Betty celebrated both her psyche's renewal and her deepened connection with her mother—wondrous gifts that she attributed to the potent love now emanating from her heart.

Performing Acts of Redemption and Salvation

The third and final phase of opening the heart consists of actions geared toward redemption and salvation. Acts of *redemption* restore deep regrets—such as "bad" choices, mistakes, painful memories, and traumatic events—to their original value. Through acts of *salvation*, we bring shattered and abandoned parts of ourselves back home. Both deeds rely on grace, or divine assistance.

Sharon was an heiress lavished early on with opulence and privilege. Yet her life had been a perpetual nightmare. She was raised by servants and nannies, sent away to boarding schools, and betrayed by adults in both settings. The man she married embezzled most of her money and on three occasions tried to murder her. Her healing began when she got off the drugs that for eight years had dulled her pain, and began owning the devastation wrought by seeing herself as a victim.

Revisiting painful memories, she learned to accept the choices she had made out of a need to feel loved, and to see that in many instances she had sacrificed her happiness and integrity. Forgiving a barrage of judgments formed early on about her self-betrayal, she emerged from the dark clouds of self-blame and delighted in her first conscious experiences of loving herself; previously she had thought of love as coming from the outside, if you were lucky. But despite her acceptance and forgiveness, Sharon still felt too damaged to move out of her victim story. Her only recourse was to embark on a relentless crusade of redemption and salvation.

She began by exploring her innermost regrets and steeping them in compassion. While lovingly nurturing her remorse about letting hurtful people into her life, she felt "saved" from the ravages of the world, protected and secure for the first time ever. She also retrieved pieces of herself she had rejected long before out of repulsion. Piece by piece, she brought these cast-off shards of herself back home, nourishing them too with love. Like the Prodigal Son returning home destitute yet celebrated, Sharon soon gleamed with the light of wholeness and inner strength, grateful for the guiding hand of grace in orchestrating her "grand reunion."

To assure herself that grace would again intervene, preventing her from creating a future as harmful as her past, she undertook a final act. She surveyed the remains of her past and declared it a barren wilderness strewn with wasted money, passion, energy, and time. Then she stepped into the mystery of her heart and asked for the promise of peace. To seal this petition, Sharon envisioned herself walking inch by inch through the charred furrows of her past, planting seeds of love. Feelings of helplessness, despair, and near hopelessness threatened to divert her, but she boldly accepted each memory, forgave the misundertandings and judgments it had spawned, and followed up with reclamation and restoration.

Grace must have answered, for very soon Sharon was diagnosed with cancer, and after a spate of anger she managed to embrace this formidable illness to further renew herself. Friends commented on the light in her eyes and the joy in her laughter.

From Sharon's perspective, these were reflections of the growth and wisdom that now sustained her. Following her recovery, she chose to live simply, valuing the loving, supportive friends who encouraged her life-enhancing decisions. Then much to her surprise, out of the newly planted seedbed of her past there sprouted inspiration to work with watercolors and share her light-imbued creations with others. Sharon had not only shed her story but blazed a trail to abundance.

Sitting in my office months later, she recounted a startling incident.

> Earlier this week I was driving on a back road with the wrong man, disappointed that he was not Mr. Wonderful, as I had hoped. I heard my mind say, *Once again you've made a mistake. You are going to have an anxiety attack.* I tried to get in touch with the old victim energy, expecting to throw an emotional fit over another poor choice. But everywhere I looked inside, I found acceptance, forgiveness, and nurturing. When I went into the place holding my first feelings about cancer, I couldn't find them. Instead, it was full of loving and the power of healing. The next thing I knew, I was blessing my life.

Blessing her life sent a clear message that Sharon no longer chose to live with the dots on the pages of her past. She had opened her heart to herself so fully that she knew *all* of life is a blessing.

When we, like Sharon, commit acts of redemption and salvation, letting go of the need to justify or dismiss earlier circumstances, we are well on our way to blessing the past no matter how excruciating it may have been. Each time we reclaim a regret and bring home an abandoned piece of ourselves, we move a step closer to a life graced with loving. Although it may take us until our last breath to heal our every hurt, the effort will bear unimaginable fruit if we see everything that comes our way as an invitation for opening our guarded hearts.

The rest is alchemy. Like the ancient wizards who sought to transmute base metals into gold, we apply an elixir and watch as nature takes its course. For us, that elixir is loving, and when we apply it to a wound through self-acceptance and self-forgiveness, we enter into an awareness of ourselves as loving beings. Following up with acts of redemption and salvation nourished by this vital contact with our divinity, we reinvigorate our original experience of wholeness. Past, present, and future are then sanctified and we become, at heart, reborn.

CHAPTER TWELVE

OBSERVING THE MIND
AND THE EMOTIONS

No amount of compassionate loving, as liberating as it is, can stop the mind and emotions from stealing our "heaven." Old mental patterns and emotional dramas, if unchecked, will continue to darken the horizon with their shenanigans, forever narrowing our field of vision and eclipsing our divine nature. Liberation from these acts of sabotage calls for vigilant observation, beginning with the mind—scriptwriter par excellence that knows just how to trigger emotional hot spots.

The Art of Mind Watching

Have you ever observed people at the park, unconcerned about what they are doing? Have you watched shoppers at the mall, without wondering whether they are happy or lonely, tired or frustrated? Have you sat in nature and watched the activity around you—the clouds drifting by, birds flying about, and butterflies flitting from one flower to the next—unattached to it all? If so, you are an adept observer. You know how to take in information without getting caught up in it.

Observing the mind, however, takes discipline, because we have a long history of engaging with our thoughts. For one thing, we are accustomed to suppressing them, overriding them, doubting them, judging them, playing "What if...?" with them, and spinning them into Oscar-winning melodramas. For another, most thoughts are inveterate pranksters.

Fortunately there are ways to cultivate the art of mind watching. In the best of circumstances, we can acknowledge a thought that arises, recognize any tendency to interact with it, and detach from that impulse, choosing to remain an observer. If we have unwittingly begun interacting with the thought, we can redirect our attention to the rising and falling of the chest that accompanies each breath, thereby disengaging from the thought and returning to observation mode. But if the mind has already lured us into one of its tricks, our only fail-safe option is to stop believing anything it says—a strategy that became necessary for thirty-five-year-old Chris.

"Your assignment for this month is to stop believing your mind," I told Chris. "Don't trust anything it tells you."

His eyes opened wide. "Don't believe my thoughts? Well, I suppose I could give it a try."

Chris, a mystery novelist, had been in counseling for months to heal a painful breakup with his lover. He had recently determined it was all for the best, and he'd begun writing again, studying bodywork, and even dating a little. Some days he felt good, but on others he daydreamed obsessively about Jim, picturing him at his favorite coffee shops, wondering if he would call, and imagining him with a new lover. As for himself, he was sure he could have been a more attentive partner and a better listener. Chris knew this obsessive fantasizing was thrusting him into his habitual Poor Me game, but he had no idea how to stop it from playing out.

His monkey mind prolonged the torment. Day and night it sent him haunting messages: *You botched the relationship. You'll never be good at intimacy. How could any man love you?* Chris, believing every word of these monologues, spiraled into despair and ill health, compounded by throbbing headaches. But he perked up at the new assignment.

The following week Chris talked about how difficult it had been to give no credence to his thoughts. "Actually, I *want* to believe them," he added. "Especially the good ones, like maybe Jim will call, or he'll want me back. But once I started believing those thoughts and they didn't come true, I ended up believing the nasty ones that followed, like, *See, he didn't call. He didn't love you after all.* I'm tired of swinging back and forth like a chandelier. How do I not believe my thoughts?"

Chris had fallen prey to the mind's favorite pastime: spinning a web of belief. The mind begins this hoax by sending out filaments of thought to capture our attention. More often than not they succeed, either because of our need to be "right" about our perceptions or because of our desperate search for answers to deep-seated quandaries. An ardent believer in his mind's messages, Chris had become hopelessly entangled in this web and needed help getting out.

"I'd suggest taking a few minutes each day to sit quietly with your thoughts. Turn off the phone ringer, set your kitchen timer, and sit comfortably on a chair or sofa. Then observe your thoughts, watching each one as if it were a leaf falling ever so slowly to the ground," I explained. "Any time you feel the urge to believe them, just notice their movement and tell yourself, 'Here they come... there they go. What a curious movie this is.'"

Chris laughed out loud. "What would my life be like if I didn't believe my thoughts?"

By the end of the month, he'd had a taste of what it might be like. With diligent practice, he had learned to disentangle himself from his mind's web of belief. His despair had lifted; his throbbing headaches were easing up; and his newfound clarity of mind had enabled him to sketch out three chapters of a new book. When I asked how he was dealing with the breakup, he replied, "I still think about Jim from time to time, but I don't obsess over it. I say,

'Oh, here's a thought about Jim. I'd like to spend the next few minutes remembering the fun we used to have, but instead I'll just let that thought flutter to the earth.'"

Dethroning the Mind

The mind's tentacles spin more than webs of damaging beliefs. They have an extensive repertoire of tricks, all geared toward holding us captive in the perception of our "smallness." While subject to the mind's reign of terror, we tell ourselves, "I am what I think." In overthrowing it, we realize we're so much more.

Yvonne, a well-respected geneticist, was brilliant. She had graduated from a prestigious university and still reveled in intellectual discussions. At parties, people gathered around her, enthralled by her quick wit. Her colleagues at work consulted with her on their most complicated problem-solving tasks, which pleased her no end since she thrived on the mental stimulation. But Yvonne refused to go anywhere her mind could not take her. She was terrified of the unknown.

She had grown up in a family that shunned meaningful conversation. Early on she sensed that something was wrong between her parents, and in time she suspected infidelity. Not knowing for sure what lay beneath their cryptic silences, she was often fearful. Yvonne compensated by excelling in school—there she felt safe and could gather all the evidence she wished. Since intelligence shielded her against fear of the unknown, she soon decided to let her mind rule her life. Once coronated, though, it brought her little joy.

When I suggested that she observe her mind, Yvonne took to the assignment as if it were a chromosomal anomaly to evaluate. But at her next session, she seemed befuddled. "At first, the observing went well," she reported. "I watched my mind map out each day in advance, helping me to fulfill everyone's expectations. Whenever it criticized my predictive abilities, as it was wont to do, I'd shrug off the comment and refocus on my stream of thoughts about the day's agenda. It was like prying into the head of a travel agent composing an elaborate itinerary."

"Then what happened?" I asked.

"The experiment bombed. Really bad feelings came up and took over my concentration. The worst of it happened as I began to think my boyfriend, Tom, was cheating on me. I felt jealous, even nauseous. Like some Pavlovian dog, I got one whiff of suspicion, felt a rush of energy, and my emotions went berserk."

"Was your mind playing tricks on you?" I asked.

"Apparently so," Yvonne said. "When I spoke with Tom that night, he assured me of his love and said there's nothing to worry about. Maybe I was tortured more by my feelings of envy than by anything having to do with our relationship. I had no idea that feelings would come trotting in with my thoughts, or that they would affect me so fiercely."

Yvonne had managed to avoid entanglement in the mind's web of belief but not in its second favorite pastime: magnetizing the emotions. This one had her in its clutches. Yvonne had so elevated her mind's seat of power that she was unable to see her emotions coming until their drama was already upon her, stressing her out. To eliminate the element of surprise, she had to either build an observation tower in her mind, which would risk isolating her from intellectual camaraderie, or dethrone her mind and thus expand her perspective. She chose the latter and set about tracking the worrisome thoughts her mind kicked up.

She began with her thoughts of Tom. Carrying an index card in her coat pocket, she would mark it each time she flashed on a disturbing speculation about him. Dozens occurred in the course of each day. "I'd be engrossed in a lab procedure and suddenly think Tom was mad at me for something I said the night before, or was ridiculing me behind my back," she remarked. "Then I'd add a line to the card and tell myself, 'There's another one.'"

After tracking a variety of perturbing thoughts, Yvonne noticed that the most upsetting ones pertained to things she had never witnessed and could not substantiate—trivialities her mind had invented. Then as she persisted in removing her mind from its place of prominence, she was able to observe her thoughts without giving them power. In the process, her stress gave way, freeing up a balanced energy she never knew she had.

One afternoon, Yvonne arrived with an impish grin. "All this 'downloading' has left room in my head for new thoughts—inspiring ideas, creative interpretations, even hunches," she said excitedly. "I have more clarity now. I feel less agitated, almost serene at times. I guess I don't need to know *everything,* or put slices of reality under the microscope to prove their existence. But I do want my mind to serve my true purpose in the world, and I suspect there is wisdom in me that exceeds my capacity to understand it. I want this wisdom in my life."

Dethroning her mind did more than eradicate Yvonne's fear of the unknown. It exposed her to other modes of knowing and to the divine intelligence at her core. Following this revelation, the dots on the page of her life receded and she saw herself not so much a decoder of genes and chromosomes as a participant in her own evolution and an embodiment of joy.

Unhooking the Emotions

Bob, a fifty-two-year-old minister, was in a spiritual quandary. Although he meditated regularly and had found considerable peace in his life, he experienced "disaster flashes" in response to scary news. For example, upon hearing that a family member was sick, he thought of them in great suffering, or terminally ill. Immediately he would develop physical symptoms—an accelerated heart rate, profuse sweating, stomach cramps, and trembling. So severe were these symptoms that he would sometimes take the afternoon off and go to bed.

His flights into doom and gloom were manageable until Bob noticed a curious pattern developing. Any time a disaster-free week slipped by, a vague sense of dread would creep into his thoughts, telling him, *Things have been going well. You'd better be wary, because something bad is about to happen.* Bob had reshocked himself so often that he had become physically addicted to the sensation of catastrophe.

The first time we met, Bob admitted that he mistook his negative fantasies for reality and got hooked on the emotions they triggered. When I asked how often his premonitions had been correct, he replied, "Well, the events themselves are never as bad as they are in my head. Maybe I play them out internally to feel the 'rush' of being alive in a quiet moment and empowered to control the outcomes, whatever they might be."

"What a huge price you are paying for this. It sounds as though you are trading in your hard-won peace," I said.

He reflected for a moment, then commented, "I do greet each day in prayer, and I experience the presence of God in my life. I wonder why I don't trust God when I hear bad news."

To unravel this mystery, Bob agreed to spend a few weeks observing the point at which his emotions latched on to information streaming from his mind, just before his body responded with sensations. We called it his "choice point"—the instant when he could elect to either continue feeding a disaster flash or unhook his emotions. Working with his choice point would set him squarely on the Self-Mastery field.

At the end of this observation period, Bob had new insights into his addiction to catastrophe. "Many times I caught myself creating a huge upset over a minor event. My emotions were so quick to hitch on to my mind's recitation that I had to literally stop what I was doing, step outside, and talk to myself."

"What did you say to yourself?" I asked.

"I assured myself that all is well, as if comforting a child who was suddenly upset. Never before have I offered myself solace. I'm beginning to think it must have come from the divine spark within me, the God I had forgotten to trust."

"So, observing your choice point helped you discharge some of that extra voltage. You became physically active, and you comforted yourself instead of catering to the disasters. What's it like living without weekly doses of catastrophe?" I asked.

Bob said that his concentration had improved dramatically, allowing him to focus on his job. He seemed delighted to be spending his afternoons peacefully at work, and not flat on his back in the throes of a disaster attack.

Perhaps you, too, have noticed how quickly energy follows thought, how rapidly depression, anxiety, or mood swings arise from unmonitored mind antics. If so, you have probably found that the more you engage with this energy, the more bodily sensations it arouses until you can say with confidence, "I am what I feel. I am a veritable dynamo, no longer empty inside. In fact, I am so charged with power I can handle anything that comes my way." But what usually comes along is unwanted symptomatology—the body's reactions to this surge of adrenaline—and before long the need for another fix.

The discovery of your choice point provides a more liberating option: you can unhook the jolting emotion and ride out its turbulence as the thought passes easily from your mind. For best results, remember that emotions are energy, much like waves in the sea. No matter how much they swell and surge, they always die down. So while riding out each wave, hold your head above water, keep breathing, and know the emotion will soon dissipate.

Remember too that emotions, like all energy, are neutral—neither good nor bad, right nor wrong. But when judged, they become positively or negatively charged, resulting in fear, blame, shame, and always contraction. By separating your feeling from any judgment of it, you will be free to surf without squandering energy in riptides of self-condemnation.

It is also true that emotions deliver messages about past hurts. A thought passing through your mind today can reactivate an emotion that was locked up inside years ago, such as self-doubt following a rejection, or despair over a loss. Hitching on to the thought, it ushers in an opportunity for you to become reacquainted with this stowaway and to realize that you are more than your wound. As you unhook the emotion, you relieve the contraction that held it in place. Then this part of you, no longer blocked, becomes a conduit for the flow of more intrinsic messages. Whispers of wisdom, heard over the fading din of self-doubt or despair, may inform you of your true purpose in life. A comforting presence, blowing in overhead, may lift your spirits. Startled into an awareness of these forces, you might ask: *What was that sound? What was that presence? Am I the observer or the observed, or both?*

Following epiphanies of this sort, most of us quietly leave the theater of mind and emotions. From our new roost in the expanded self, we are able to see how futile the old recycled feelings and sensations actually are. So it is that in choosing to unhook rather than indulge tempestuous emotions, we achieve a new level of consciousness. Simultaneously we free up this energy for growth-promoting ventures.

The World beyond Mind and Emotions

Stewart, laid off after twenty years of employment at a large computer firm, knew just what he wanted to do. His dream was to start a computer company of his own, offering high-quality customer service and professional expertise. Stewart had been studying spiritual principles for some time and hoped to implement them in service to his new clients. But even though he knew how devious the mind and emotions could be, they soon got the better of him and began orchestrating a painful inner reality. He wrestled daily with self-doubt, anxiety, negative mind chatter, and mood swings.

"I've got to have God as my partner in this business venture or I won't be able to do it," he confided one afternoon. "It's huge. There's too much I need to learn."

"God as your *partner*?" I asked. "What does that mean to you?"

"That I am supported inwardly to go for my dream. You see, my mind tells me I don't know what I'm doing, and my anxiety insists that I'll fail. With God as my partner, I won't need to waste precious energy on these matters. I'll just focus on each new task and know that everything will unfold perfectly."

To avoid further engagement with his intrusive thoughts and anxieties, Stewart devised a practice for using them as reminders of his new business partner. Any time a thought lured him into obsessing over time or money, he would ask himself, *Is this a real concern or some mental script?* Whenever he woke up vexed with anxiety, he treated himself to nurturing, comforting statements. In moments of not knowing what to do next, he deferred to his divinity's instructions, which were always simple and practical, such as *It's a good time to make that call* or *Why not compose a mission statement?* Occasionally, Stewart had to wait patiently for his instructions.

"After all these years in a top-down corporate structure, it's thrilling to rely on inner direction," he informed me after a few weeks of dedicated practice. "Already I've gotten a business license, placed a deposit on office space, purchased the start-up furniture and equipment, hired a top-notch staff, and more. Oddly, I've hardly had to use my mind at all. I'm just dealing with whatever is needed, one task at a time. And every day, small miracles happen, like a sign arriving unexpectedly to be installed over the door, and a used compact refrigerator needing a new home. Of course, I give my business partner full credit for these unsolicited items.

"The few times I was snagged by obsession, I took an 'observation break.' Sure enough, I found the culprit was either my mind shifting into a perception of lack or some hooked-on emotion whirling me into stress."

Stewart went on to describe how he was learning to trust Spirit in this new context. He claimed it was even infusing his family life with peace, joy, and fulfillment. Then he smiled broadly and announced that his business partner had given him a day off in honor of his steadfast devotion.

Stewart, for his part, recognized that he had indeed completed a right of passage from an inner hell to an inner heaven. He handed me a document he had prepared to mark the occasion of his release from bondage to the mind and emotions. It read:

Figure 12–1

MY DECLARATION OF INDEPENDENCE

I hereby resolve to never again become enslaved to my thoughts and feelings. I will seek counsel only from Spirit. If ever I happen to slip back into my earlier state of inner hell, I vow to recapture my freedom by working with the corresponding practice noted below.

Inner Hell	Inner Heaven
Contraction	Expansion
Control	Openheartedness
Oppression	A safe place within
Self-doubt	Self-acceptance
Self-judgment	Self-forgiveness
Self-punishment	Redemption and salvation
Mental tricks/	Observation
Emotional dramas	
Anxiety	Trust

The world beyond mind and emotions, our inner heaven, is the dwelling place of our divine essence. Like a clear mountain stream flowing eternally with fresh runoff, this essence washes away cobwebs of illusion and provides ongoing nourishment and renewal. Although undemanding of our attention, it imparts wisdom each time we come to its banks and ask, *What is the truth I am seeking?*

You will know you have sipped of its waters if in shifting your focus from thoughts and feelings you sense a sudden alignment with your unique sense of purpose, an instinctual awareness that you are on track and supported, a surprising sense of ease, and a guidance you can trust. Like the young knight Parsifal in Wolfram von Eschenbach's early-thirteenth-century Grail legend, you need not be on a quest in order to discover your true identity.

But having tapped into it, you will gaze upon the world with new eyes and a wholeness of vision, for the unmanifest has become manifest.

Our awareness expands exponentially through contact with our divinity. It assures us there is no lack of providence, that even the bountiful stream of wisdom at the center of our being has been and always will be available to us. It also informs us that we are someone very special beyond what we think or feel, and that who we are can shape the outcome of any path we choose to take.

CHAPTER THIRTEEN

WALKING WITH FEAR

After prying off its masks, even seasoned liberation aficionados are stopped in their tracks by fear. Danger strikes, habit rears its pernicious head, and the heart shuts down. On some days it spends more time closed than open, a victim of fear's paralyzing sting.

Have you ever found yourself speaking candidly and then freezing in midsentence, suddenly concerned about disapproval or rejection? Have you curled up peacefully with a book on a Saturday night and, partway into chapter 3, begun wondering what your friends are doing and if you've been left out of the weekend festivities? Did you ever suspend promising negotiations on the sale of your business, or evacuate a perfectly delightful intimate relationship? Do new groups make you nervous, or unfamiliar places give you "butterflies"? In observing the emotions that bring you to a standstill, you may discover that a major fear or two is governing your life.

The Unwritten Laws of Fear

Fear is a harsh ruler with one command: *Stop. Do not trespass or you'll be hurt.* The moment we approach a hot spot of fear, everything tells us not to proceed. The mind, emotions, and body all conspire to make us "small" again and keep us contracted.

We respond instinctively, and for good reason: we have been well conditioned. Our conditioning began at a very early age with warnings *(Don't play with the next-door neighbors, because they are not like us)*, threats *(Don't upset your parents or you'll be in trouble)*, and expectations *(You'd better get good grades on your report card)*. It continued over the next decade or two with advice *(Buy this deodorant so the girls will swarm around you)*, admonitions *(What self-respecting person would have such a dingy floor?)*, and injunctions *(Don't break up the family; you made your bed, now lie in it)*.

These messages and others came from our environment, which provided us with an entire roster of acceptable behaviors. Departures from them seemed to exact such heavy tolls that we did our best to conform. Over time, as the messages were either consciously or subliminally internalized, they became etched in our minds as if engraved on sacred clay tablets. Simultaneously, the accompanying reactive states were programmed into our emotions and our bodies.

Worse, the laws of fear were so deeply etched in our minds that we formed a web of beliefs about the consequences we would suffer for breaking them. These penalties were exceedingly severe, ensuring that we would not tread where fear did not want us to go. See figure 13–1, on page 117, for a sample listing of these laws and the beliefs they spawned.

Unlike the laws that govern civil liberties, the flow of traffic, and property rights, the laws of fear have no firm foundation, no real purpose. They were inventions handed down by individuals who were themselves recipients of them. Most likely, the decrees were conjured up centuries ago by people living in fear of political or religious persecution. Despite their fictitious nature, however, we respond to these laws out of our conditioning. And in doing so, we lose track of who we are, what we are doing, and where we are going.

YOU CAN MAKE IT HEAVEN

Figure 13–1

Ten Commandments of Fear	Beliefs
1. Thou shalt not make mistakes.	*I'll be punished.*
2. Thou shalt not trust thyself or others.	*I'll look like a fool.*
3. Thou shalt not let down thy guard.	*I'll lose my power.*
4. Thou shalt not ask for help.	*I'll be disappointed.*
5. Thou shalt not take risks.	*I won't be safe.*
6. Thou shalt not express unpleasant feelings.	*I'll be rejected.*
7. Thou shalt not follow thy passion.	*I'll be abandoned.*
8. Thou shalt not take care of thyself.	*I'll be seen as selfish.*
9. Thou shalt not succeed.	*I'll feel my unworthiness.*
10. Thou shalt not seek the truth.	*I'll perish in the vast unknown.*

Eddie's boss asked to meet with him the next day about his job performance. Eddie's stomach lurched. As he drove home, his conditioned response to the fear of making a mistake began its litany: *I've done something wrong. I should have looked over that last report one more time. I'm going to lose my job. How will I pay my bills? What will my friends say?* While pulling up to his driveway, he broke into a chorus of judgments: *I always mess things up. Dad was right—I won't ever amount to anything. I just won't get ahead.* Following his fill of self-deprecation, he turned against his presumed tormentor: *My boss doesn't care how many hours I've socked into this job, or how many golf games I've given up. He's never appreciated my work. Who does he think he is?!*

In a matter of twenty minutes, Eddie's emotions had swung from anxiety to anger, panic, and resentment. He stumbled in the door reeling from stomach cramps and a backache, and kicked the first chair in sight. To regain control over his behavior, he self-medicated.

Eddie was suffering from more than a shut-down heart; his mind, emotions, and body had staged a full-fledged attack on his sense of reality. His conditioned response to this law of fear was so pronounced that it had distorted his perceptions. Like walking into a House of Mirrors, he beheld only skewed images of himself. And with each one, he became more disoriented until he lost sight of the truth and saw only the dots on the page of his life.

Confronting the Illusion of Danger

So charged is the conditioned response to fear that often the only way to neutralize it is by inching up for a firsthand look at the bogus danger underneath it. This can be a vigorous expedition.

To approach a fear, you must wend your way through a maze of habitual excuses, rationalizations, and accusations, riding out each emotion they stir up. Wracked by an anguishing sense of uncertainty and fragility while just inches away, you may think, *Surely I am about to encounter a cruel dark demon.* But alas, this instant of heightened vulnerability is a defining moment, giving you an opportunity to choose your course: Will you succumb to contraction once again or will you open your heart to the fear and bathe it with love? Once permeated with love, that clay tablet begins to dissolve, revealing that in fact there was no danger lurking behind it. You will emerge harboring a mere relic of the old fear, replenished by the great stores of energy that had been holding it in place, and stripped of the illusion of danger.

Judy, a successful health-care practitioner, had taken major strides in healing her childhood wounds. With compassion and loving, she had come to terms with the long-ago death of her baby brother, her relative lack of contact with a workaholic father, and the burden of caring for her frequently bedridden mother. Judy had also broken free of the drug and alcohol binges she had gone on as a young adult to quiet the "monsters that lived in the dark recesses" of her psyche. But taught as a child never to think about scary things, she was now certain that any attention given to these monsters would unleash all manner of destruction. Despite her dedication to self-mastery, whenever she was scared Judy capitulated to her family mandate not to face fear. Avoidance and denial seemed to be encoded in every cell of her body.

One day she complained of mounting fatigue. Eating and sleeping well had not managed to ward off hours of daily exhaustion.

"What seems to be draining your energy?" I asked. "Have you been working overtime ignoring those monsters?"

"No, I just blot them out of my mind," she said, suddenly nonchalant.

"And they go away?"

"Well, for a while they do. But then they come back," she admitted. "I've also been feeling a clutching in my chest, and an occasional stiffness in my neck. At times I break out in a panicky sweat for no reason."

"It sounds like something is making these fears very powerful. Do you think your avoidance of them might actually be feeding them?"

"I don't know, but I do seem to be working harder these days to stave them off."

"If that's so, and if the fears are being fed by your avoidance and held captive your denial, what would be a good remedy?"

"It's hard to say. I've had my fill of pain and terror over the years, and dealing with these monsters head-on seems much too dangerous. Besides, I've lost track of what they're about. I think I'm just fearful of fear."

Judy agreed to spend the week contemplating a new possibility: that by letting herself *experience* a fear, she might find there is nothing to be afraid of. At the very least, she said, this might redirect her energy flow and help alleviate her fatigue.

When she returned the following week, she seemed perkier. But she was troubled by recurring nightmares.

"Something big keeps chasing me," she reported, nearly breathless with apprehension. "I can't see it, but I know it's huge and I have to run fast to get away from it."

"Could it be an inner truth trying to capture your attention?" I suggested.

"If there is a *truth* inside me to examine, then I want to know about it," she said eagerly. "I will do my best to stop running from this relentless pursuer."

The nightmares soon ended, and so did Judy's desire to flee from fear. She gradually became more vulnerable to her inner world and began talking about scary events that occurred in her day-to-day life. Telling herself the truth each time she experienced fear, and forgiving herself for having the fear, eventually gave her conscious control over her long-conditioned response. When in the grip of fear, she no longer defaulted to avoidance and denial.

In fact, she began surrendering to her fears, naming them, even offering them comfort and reassurance. She told them they didn't have to hide anymore, that everything was okay. With her illusion of danger dispelled, she felt increasingly at ease interacting with these parts of herself. The more attention she gave them, the more their intensity diminished, and the more her sense of empowerment expanded.

One afternoon Judy arrived at her appointment radiant with energy. "The strangest thing just happened," she announced. "I was talking lovingly to a giant fear I named Weakosaurus. And do you know what she did? She leaped into my palm and shrunk to the size of a lizard! I was on my way to the car, so I just kept moving. And I had to giggle, because there I was walking along with my number one fear in my hand instead of coursing through my body."

Walking Through Fear

Carlos, a successful restaurateur, lived with his wife and three children in West Texas. A longtime student of world religions, he hungered for answers to life's deepest mysteries. Lately he had become distracted, quietly pondering his purpose. The restaurant staff began commenting on the glazed-over look in his eyes. His family remarked on his unusual sullenness and played hide-and-seek with his dry sense of humor, trying to elicit a smile. Carlos himself had noticed a quiet tension settling into his shoulders and jaw.

As he stepped into my office on his fifty-fifth birthday, he appeared agitated. He was a fortunate man, he said. His business was prospering and his family meant the world to him. But he felt stuck in quicksand and didn't know how to get out.

"What do you suppose is sucking you in?" I asked Carlos, half suspecting that the occasion of his birthday had ushered in a life inventory of some sort.

"I feel like I'm serving a sentence, like I'm not living purposefully, in the most meaningful way possible," he replied, his eyes downcast.

"What's holding you back from going after what you truly want?"

"I can't seem to budge. I grew up with an unspoken edict: Thou shalt not get second chances," he said, looking me directly in the eye. "I've always believed I would not survive a mistake, and now I am confident that the universe enforces this decree and dispenses punishment for any breach of contract. So rather than risk making a wrong move, I play it safe."

"If you knew you had a second chance, what would you attempt to do?"

"My greatest wish would be to live in a forgiving universe, a place of lightness, buoyancy, joy, happiness, and peace. I want to hang out in a universe where I'm accepted just the way I am, where I can fall and get up again instead of thinking I'll crash and burn in eternal damnation.

"You see, the problem is not about *what I do;* my outer life couldn't be better. This darkness I feel is about *who I am.* And right now I am Carlos the Impeccable Robot performing eight hundred deeds a day, and my heart's not in any of them. I don't even know where it is anymore. So, if I got a second chance I would climb out of this muck and move as unflinchingly as possible to a place that recognizes the benevolence of all creation, accepts its perfection no matter how flawed it may be, and offers unmerited divine assistance. It's a paradise I've probably read about, but not one I'm personally aware of." He let out a long sigh.

"It sounds like a cosmos permeated with grace," I offered, "where fear is comforted and judgments are forgiven."

"Yeah, nice place," he grumbled, still immersed in his distorted image of himself.

"I wonder how close you might come to this place by choosing to live under the canopy of its beneficent blessings instead of under a punitive law. Grace or fear—it's all about choice, don't you think?"

Carlos looked stunned. He liked the idea that living under the jurisprudence of law is not a sentence but a choice. He enjoyed toying with the notion that in response to childhood experiences, *he* had drafted the law about second chances, had elected to be governed by it, had appointed the universe to enforce it, and was now in the throes of a conditioned response to it, complete with prescriptive judgments. Still, he could not picture himself making a new choice and having it work. He lacked evidence. He felt powerless. He did not deserve a bounteous life.

As a birthday present to himself, the first ever, Carlos promised to begin digging out of the quicksand enough to someday choose a new form of self-governance and ultimately shift his perception. For the next several weeks, he would perform actions and deeds in the spirit of loving rather than fearing. He would regard the universe as an ally and seek signs of its support in whatever small things came his way—fresh asparagus to feature on his dinner menu, a tender phone call from his wife smoothing out a stressful moment in his day, a game of catch with his children. He would give himself second, third, and fourth chances, no matter what. In addition, he would strive to be more spontaneous and, in turn, welcome unforeseen circumstances as revelations that he could indeed expand into a grace-filled existence.

It must have been the perfect gift, because very soon Carlos began feeling more light-hearted and energetic. His interactions with others had fewer "disconnects," as he put it. And his tension had given way to long interludes of serenity. "My heart has been making unsolicited guest appearances lately," he noted. "I seem to come to peace when my heart and mind are congruent."

Months later, when his fear had significantly diminished, Carlos had a breakthrough dream in which he visited his grandmother's two-story house. As a child, he had loved the living room, its windows stretching from floor to ceiling, catching the summer breeze. His favorite spot was the attic, where he would rummage through old suitcases, furniture, baby clothes, and photographs.

Recounting his dream, Carlos said:

I enter from the front porch and immediately notice that the entire first story is under construction. Walls have been torn down; the floor is strewn with chunks of plaster. Surprisingly I don't stop to investigate the rubble of the living room I once knew so well. Instead, I tromp through and head straight for the stairs to the attic. For some reason the doorway to the attic is tiny, so on hands and knees I crawl through what turns into a dark passageway. Once out the other side, I stand up and gasp. The formerly dingy and musty room, cluttered with deteriorating memorabilia, is now a beautiful, light-filled chamber free of everything but floor, walls, and a most unusual ceiling. The wood floor gleams. The walls are inscribed with ancient scrollwork suggestive of hidden knowledge. And the ceiling is the sky, drawing my gaze forever upward toward an expanse that seems to welcome me. My heart fills with joy.

Carlos's dream had led him to a place inside himself that, unbeknownst to him, had been under construction all this time. Every step he took to climb out of his limited belief system had chipped away at the fear holding it in place. Meanwhile grace, starting upstairs, had overseen the remodeling of his childhood refuge, enabling Carlos to traipse through the demolition and stand tall in the universe he had envisioned. Now liberated from fear, he could claim this place as his own every day of his life.

So it is for us all. Opening to grace, we can walk through any fear and emerge in an inner chamber suffused with cosmic abundance. This is the dwelling place of grace, the home of our divinity. Here we bow only to blessings.

Figure 13–2

TEN BLESSINGS OF GRACE

1. You will discover rewards in every moment of opening your heart.

2. You will know that all your experiences are growth promoting.

3. You will find empowerment in expansion.

4. You will receive in great measure while attending to your purpose.

5. You will feel assisted in times of challenge.

6. You will experience acceptance in being honest.

7. You will uncover your purpose through loving.

8. You will increase your compassion for others each time you come home to yourself.

9. You will realize that you are here to prosper.

10. You will live in joy while seeking the divinity within you.

YOU CAN MAKE IT HEAVEN

CHAPTER FOURTEEN

PLEDGING LOYALTY TO THE SELF

The hidden self that comes into view on the Self-Mastery playing field needs our allegiance and faithful attention. Sustained by this steady stream of devotion, it furnishes the mind with new insights and the emotions with fresh vigor. We become aware of an inner domain, now cleared of fear, that is receptive to energy flowing through the outer world and is equipped to establish meaningful links with other people. At last we can access our truth. Having let go of a painful past, we can also share this truth with others and reap the joys of open, honest communication. Suddenly connection is everywhere—in disagreements with our partner, in playful abandon with our children, and on walks alone at sunset.

Pledging loyalty to this self, however, can be formidable. For starters, you may not recognize yourself. Like the butterfly emerging from its cocoon, you are no longer anything like who you thought you were, making it difficult to know quite where to place your loyalty. Then, too, familiar voices can weaken your resolve. Inner voices may insinuate that you have wandered too far afield, or warn you to hurry back to safety. Outer ones, vehemently disapproving, may chide you for changing too much or threaten to disassociate from you.

It can be tempting to succumb. You may be used to overriding your interests for the sake of others—abdicating to the wishes of loved ones, and compromising when friends seem displeased or angry. Or an unmet need of your own might begin drawing your allegiance away from the new you and injecting concerns about leaving the security of your old cocoon.

Myriad tugs on our attention dissuade us from pledging loyalty to the new self. But in turning away from our essence, we stumble off the Self-Mastery field and land with a thump on the old Foiled Again pitch.

Caving In to Guilt

John, a highly successful businessman in his late sixties, was hoping to retire. He and Carol, his wife of forty years, had spent the summer alternately traveling abroad and visiting their children and grandchildren on the West Coast. During that time, John began turning inward and finding parts of himself that yearned to come to expression.

"I want to study Asian brush calligraphy. I'd love to work with my hands for a change," he told me. "I'd also like to offer a class or two to entrepreneurs, maybe at the community college."

"What exciting prospects—a dedication to the real you," I said. "What does Carol think of these ideas?"

"Well," he said sheepishly, "I haven't mentioned them—never even told her I'd like to retire. You see, she's got her eye on a million-dollar home in the foothills. She thinks it would be a perfect spot for the kids to visit, that we worked hard to get to this point in our lives, that we really ought to buy the place. But between you and me, I do not want to keep up that kind of mortgage."

When I encouraged him to share his feelings with Carol and arrive at a mutually agreeable solution, he replied, "You know, she really deserves that house. Maybe I do, too. There's no reason to retire now. What's a few more years?"

"Are you afraid to tell Carol you'd like to retire? Are you worried about her reaction?"

"I'd hate to make her unhappy. She'll withdraw and refuse to speak to me for days. I can't stand that feeling of rejection. It would be easier to give her what she wants. I refuse to lose my marriage."

"What about the parts of you that would like to learn brushwork and want to give back to others through teaching? Service in the world is an important conduit for the flow of gratitude and love."

John shook his head slowly. "There might be time for that later. The last thing I want to do now is see disappointment on Carol's face. It always makes me feel guilty."

"Is that Carol's disappointment you see or your own? Are you perhaps projecting onto *her* the guilt you feel for betraying parts of *yourself?*" I asked.

John conceded that his loyalty was caught in a tug-of-war between his wife's dreams and his inner call for growth. But in the end he went along with Carol's wishes. He felt he had no choice, and he was unschooled in the consequences of abandoning parts of himself.

Before long he was better educated. One Saturday months after our last session, I chanced upon a very weary John at the neighborhood market. "We bought the house and my wife is happy as a clam," he reported, his voice thick with resignation. "I'm still lumbering off to work—and plan to keep at it, God willing. I guess my golden years have turned a muddy brown."

Caving in to guilt is always an option. To appease its early twinges, we often pledge ourselves to acts of counterfeit self-sacrifice, hoping they will win us approval from others and sanctuary from rejection. Ironically, in doing so we abandon the creative urges deep within that help us come alive. Then right away we are back to the old win-lose game plan, seeing another person triumph at our expense . . . all because loyalty to ourselves was too uncomfortable.

Most often, we don't even think of loyalty when faced with an apparent conflict of wishes. We instinctively tell ourselves, *Not now, maybe later,* and turn away from the matter, shutting down before the pain of self-abandonment fully reaches our awareness. But over time, one minor disloyalty after another can silence the call to self-expression.

Stretching for a Win-Win Tango

Clare's voice was panicky on the phone. "I recently met a guy on the Internet. There was instant rapport, really deep. But when I don't hear from him, I lose it. I don't understand what's going on—after all these months of tuning in to me, I link up with Miguel and come apart. Any time I log on and find no mail from him, I break out in a cold sweat."

"What part of you are you dishonoring?" I asked.

"Probably the part that tells me I'm going too fast. I'm so focused on Miguel, on what he wants and how he seems to tick, that I forget about me. But I'm afraid that if I slow down he'll get away. I've had enough men vanish on me, and I definitely want this one in my life."

"What happens inside when you override the urge to slow down?"

"It feels like I'm betraying a part of me I've learned to trust. I get shaky, as though I'm standing on fragile ground."

As we continued the conversation, Clare began to back up enough to see the cause for her breach in loyalty: the answer to an unfulfilled need was parading around as a "dream come true." The love and devotion she needed to give herself had galloped into her life like a prince on a white steed, challenging her hard-won commitment to self-mastery. As much as Clare did not want to risk losing her prince, she also knew the value of honoring all parts of her essence, so she decided to slow down.

Over the next few weeks, Clare gently reestablished a connection with herself while communicating with Miguel, all the while braving the discomfort over possibly losing him. In letters to him, she began sharing her doubts about intimacy and her past disappointments with men. He welcomed these revelations and told her about similar experiences he'd had with women, remarking on how easy it is to get lost in another person.

Each time she focused on staying connected inside, Clare felt less and less scared. She also discovered that her panic over losing Miguel had in fact been externalized terror over losing herself. "I feel more empowered than ever in this relationship," she stated. "The part that so desperately wanted the right man to come along and complete me is very happy having *me* perform this job. I can finally trust me to take care of myself."

I marveled at her willingness to stretch from "I'd better not express myself with this person since he might not like who I am" to "I'm not being totally honest. Let me begin again." A forty year old accustomed to pleasing others and telling them what they want to hear, Clare had always felt off balance in partnerships. And here she was, being microscopically honest in an effort to remain loyal to her self with this man. Surely she's headed for win-win blessings this time around. These were the thoughts passing through my head when the phone rang.

"Guess what?" It was Clare, beaming. "Miguel and I are going to *meet*—in romantic Martha's Vineyard, over the December holidays. It just might be my first whirl into heaven with a partner. Or at least it seems that way, because trust and safety are not up for barter. Miguel and I honor all the parts of ourselves and each other, and every day online or by phone, we celebrate our allegiance to both. This must have been a gift from the angels!"

It may well have been. Many people describe encounters with angels-in-disguise along the sidelines of the Self-Mastery playing field. It is said that they hide their wings under a cloak of skepticism, disapproval, mild threats, and doubt. They call us out for drills to see how well we are handling our loyalty to the self and to help us strengthen our weak points. Then they champion our best efforts.

The angels on the sidelines conduct these drills so surreptitiously that we rarely know we are being tested. Typically, they step onto the field in the guise of well-meaning people in our lives, and issue pleas or threats. They may appear as a spouse *(Sacrifice everything for my happiness)*, a lover *(Give me all your attention)*, a family member *(What would your dearly departed father say?)*, a friend *(Stay just the way you've always been)*, even a group or organization *(Toe the party line no matter what)*. The angels then return to the sidelines to watch our performance.

If we are consciously pursuing self-mastery and eager to stay on the field, we may suddenly see ourselves through their eyes. We may even ask ourselves a few questions to evaluate our progress (see figure 14-1).

Figure 14–1

SELF-MASTERY PROGRESS REPORT

Am I ready to:

❧ Take responsibility for my life and forgive and bless everything in my past?

❧ Release outgrown forms of safety and security?

❧ Tell myself the microscopic truth in every moment?

❧ Extend compassion to myself and others?

❧ Say "yes" to discovering the source of my abundance?

❧ Be loving at every opportunity?

Who are these angels, and what do they want from us? An experience with any one of them is like a meeting with the "guardian of the threshold" known to European mystery schools of the eighteenth, nineteenth, and twentieth centuries, and like the *nagual* in shamanic traditions. It is an encounter with an intimidating being who stands at the threshold into the realm of secret knowledge. The embodiments the angels take on are reminiscent of the "double"—the Jungian shadow, the German *doppelganger*, or the French *concierge*—appearing to seekers in a crucial moment of self-confrontation.

But unlike their folkloric counterparts, the angels on the sidelines are our cheerleaders and our familiars, commissioned to usher us through the dots of our reality and into the hidden realms. They understand that without a firm commitment to all parts of the newly revealed self, we cannot learn to trust ourselves, and without trust we cannot continue expanding. These angels know who we are. They see who we can become. And they want the very best for us.

Honoring the Voices Within

Pledging loyalty to the new self can spark a revolt unless measures are taken to temper the meddlesome voices that have enjoyed our rapt attention all these years. We know them well, both individually and as a chorus, sometimes an uninvited glee club. There is the basso profundo who booms, *Don't lose control,* over and over again; the baritone bellowing, *The victim winds are blowing in;* the tenor chanting, *To the rescue you must go;* the alto's notorious glissando, *Beware the tides of rejection;* the soprano's *Some day your prince will come;* and many more. Since these choristers like to be honored, they may not agree to eternal silence, but they will consent to peaceful negotiations.

To proceed, announce a summit conference and invite their conductor to come speak on their behalf. Their conductor is your ego, whose job it is to keep you running at peak performance. Plan on welcoming a rather down-in-the-mouth ego, grumpy about the encounter and feeling threatened by your recent expansion. Then strive for a win-win outcome, following this script if you wish:

YOU: Thank you for coming. I wanted to bring you up-to-date on the recent shift in attention. I've decided to move beyond limitation and I'd like your help.

EGO: Well, I want *you* to know I'm not happy about this. It's *me* that should have the attention. I've spent years cultivating this personality you call your chorus. I've made sure they would cover all the bases and have you looking good, enjoying life's comforts, and feeling safe and secure.

YOU: You've done a superb job. My personality has kept me humming along just fine in most instances. I appreciate your perseverance in "looking out for number one." But this field of Self-Mastery requires me to let go of control and trust an emerging part of me that will be running the show from now on.

EGO: Humph, so who am I supposed to give my baton to?

YOU: A part of me that knows how to take charge without inducing fear. A part that allows new voices to solo and to compose their own refrains as needed. The general tempo will be less hurried and there will be a broader spectrum of tones, some of which you might consider off-key. This new conductor, my inner guide, will need your cooperation during the transition.

EGO: It sounds to me like I'll be on the street in no time. And after decades of such dedicated service!

YOU: Actually, you will remain a power player. You'll be installed as director of the chorus, responsible for interpolating each score so that the voices can learn their new parts in maintaining self-esteem and discipline.

EGO: How am I to know what these new arrangements will sound like, assuming I can hear them at all?

YOU: I will be sending you clear signals from time to time— intentions that I'll be setting. I may set an intention for openheartedness, for instance, or for acceptance, forgiveness, peace, abundance, or loving.

EGO: And what good will it do me to hold this intention?

YOU: Basically, you won't have to work so hard. We'll be mut-
ing the fear stanzas, especially the two-by-fours, the mind
chatter, and the wail of stuck emotions.

EGO: For years I've been looking for something to keep those
guys in line. They're always messing up verses and coming
in on the wrong beat. If intention can stop that, I'm all for
it. And what's this new conductor in charge of?

YOU: Growth and revelation. My inner guide hears anthems as
yet unknown to me that have been with me from the start.
The music and words are all original, but you need never
fret about being judged for getting them wrong. Just hold
the intention and the voices will follow your lead, in harmony and balance. You will be even more efficient at
organizing and mediating... and graceful as well.

EGO: Now you're talking my language—my job gets easier and
I look good at the same time! I'm ready to try this intention thing.

At the end of the summit conference, begin mastering the art
of setting an intention. This is the final step in tempering the voices that might otherwise rebel.

An intention is a clear focus on an inner attribute that you
would like to amplify. This clarity of focus then directs mental,
emotional, physical, and spiritual energy toward the desired attribute, ultimately fulfilling your intention. While working with
intention, understand that it differs from a goal; whereas a goal
pertains to something that does not yet exist, an intention refers to
something that does but is not yet fully realized.

To be effective, an intention must be *consciously set,* because
simply deciding to focus on an attribute may not galvanize the
necessary energy. For example, suppose you decide to go inside and
connect with your divinity through meditation, contemplation,

prayer, or a spiritual exercise. You find a comfortable place to sit, turn off the phone ringer, and shut the door. Then you close your eyes, take a deep breath, and relax. Immediately your thoughts wander off, going over your grocery list, replaying last night's conversation with your partner, flashing on a pair of cowboy boots you saw in a shop window downtown. To bring your attention back, you will need to set an intention, such as "I am connecting with my divinity." This is a statement the ego can hear and the distracting inner voices can respond to. With practice, all thoughts, feelings, and physical sensations unrelated to your intention will fall away.

Every aspect of pledging loyalty to the true self brings exciting returns. Interactions with others launch visible growth spurts. Negotiations with ourselves transform sabotaging impulses into allies willing to perform in concert with the rest. Once free enough to connect inwardly, we begin to create an intentional reality. In fact, each time we set an intention another piece of the true self becomes illuminated from within and reflected out into the world.

CHAPTER FIFTEEN

TUNING IN TO AWARENESS

The labor of liberation is sweetened by the blessings of awareness. These bring us knowledge about who we really are, certainty that we're free to be ourselves, and relief from wanting things to be other than they are. But awareness turned inward, like a toddler on wobbly legs, needs attention and lots of practice. In response, it deepens.

The notion that human awareness deepens has been slow to enter the doors of perception. Although we are a culture prone to measurement—as evidenced in pollen counts, barometric pressures, heart rates, cholesterol levels, IQ scores, body mass indexes, weights, and heights—rarely do we take note of the gains in awareness. Yet the fact remains that the more attention we give to awareness, the more aware we become.

Tuning in to awareness has immediate benefits as well, since it divulges important information. It shows us the roadblocks inside that have us feeling obstructed on the outside. It exposes the internal quakes that we experience as external chaos, and the newly restored pathways of connection that help us perceive the world as a friendlier place. In each instance, we come away realizing that what we were looking for in the outer world are needs of an *inner* ecosystem yearning to be cleared of debris and emptied of nonindigenous beliefs so it can reveal itself as the rich habitat that it truly is.

A deepened awareness of the inner landscape provides an additional benefit: ongoing revelations of our divine nature. These revelations treat us to the alchemical handiwork of loving, the awesome labors of grace, and periodically a surprise visit from wisdom updating us on our life's purpose.

So it is that as we replace unconscious habits with receptivity to the newness of each moment, awareness helps us catch up with ourselves. This form of intelligence gathering is so vital that it warrants as much attention as we can give it, arranging for "time in" as readily as we do time out. The best way to stay current with inner world events is by tuning in at least once a day.

The pages that follow present seven awareness exercises that can help you press beyond the insights you have already gleaned. These exercises provide hands-on experience with liberation techniques mentioned in previous chapters. Each one opens with an intention, which for best results can be repeated several times in any day, and closes with an Awareness Update containing points to consider while recording your new insights. You might enjoy dating these observations, entering them in a notebook labeled "Awareness Journal," and using them to track your deepening revelations.

Work with these exercises in any way you wish. You may want to concentrate on a different one each day of the week, repeating the sequence in weeks to come. Or you might prefer to work with one exercise extensively before moving on to the next. In either case, begin with the most relevant exercise and follow up in any order that seems helpful. From time to time, salute the power of your intentions and the deepening of your awareness.

Awareness Exercise #1

TAKING LIFE LESS PERSONALLY

Shifting perspective from "Everything is about me" to "This is not about me" shows just how often the mind can be our worst enemy. When you observe your thoughts rather than identify with them, you begin to see beyond the mind to the true self. [*Note*: At first, work with this exercise in a quiet spot for a designated period of time. With experience, you will be able to do it while driving, showering, or washing the dishes.]

Intention: *I am observing my thoughts.*

Procedure

- Notice the thoughts passing through your mind—the judgments, insistence on being right, mind chatter, speculations about unworthiness or lack, and other limiting beliefs.

- Watch each one as if it were a cloud drifting across the sky or a leaf falling to the ground.

- Tell yourself, "Here's a thought about _____," making sure not to judge it.

- Remind yourself that you are more than these thoughts.

Awareness Update

- Record your experience.

    What inner shifts did you notice while observing your thoughts?

Awareness Exercise #2

UNFASTENING STUCK EMOTIONS

To step back from a feeling is to see it for what it is—pure energy. Since energy is normally in motion, it stirs up a storm while stuck inside. Each time you unfasten a stuck emotion, you prevent entrapment in worry, guilt, or depression.

Intention: *I am observing this feeling as energy.*

Procedure

- Notice a feeling welling up within you—anxiety, hurt, disappointment, sadness, resentment, shame and blame, or any other intense emotion.

- Determine where it is situated in your body. Then tell yourself, "This feeling of _____ in my _____ is energy."

- Walk around a bit and observe the energy beginning to flow.

- Observe the triggering thought to find out what it wants to do with this feeling. Does it want to obsess over it, produce a drama, brew an anger fit, or let it go?

- To let it go, find your choice point—the spot where the feeling attached to the thought—taking care not to judge the feeling.

- Unhook the feeling and ride it like a wave to shore.

- Acknowledge that you are more than this feeling.

Awareness Update

- Record your experience.
  What changes did you notice while observing the energy of your feeling?

Awareness Exercise #3

LISTENING INWARDLY WITH COMPASSION

A hurt, disappointment, anger, and fear all signal that a part of the inner world feels neglected. In listening compassionately to its grievance, you learn about the nature of feelings and begin to open your heart to yourself.

Intention: *I am opening my heart.*

Procedure

- Create a blame-free zone inside, and allow any upset part of you to come and speak freely.

- Invite your compassionate observer to accept the grievances and to offer comfort.

- If the upset part expresses a judgment, lovingly pardon the underlying misunderstanding, saying, "I forgive myself for making this judgment." [*Note:* If your forgiveness does not immediately release the anguish, repeat this practice. With each repetition your heart will open wider, gradually relieving the pain.]

- Appreciate your heart's active involvement in accepting and forgiving this anguishing part of you that was previously too fearful of reproach to voice its pain.

Awareness Update

- Record your experience.
   What judgments needed to be forgiven?
   What subtle shifts occurred in your self-esteem as you opened your heart to yourself?

Awareness Exercise #4

RELEASING THE PAST

The heart shuts down when it is flooded with regrets or with memories of loss, betrayal, abandonment, abuse, and other incidents seemingly too painful to be revisited. When the chambers are gently unlocked and the past is let go, this vital organ can once again serve as an unlimited source of loving. [*Note:* Letting go of a painful past takes practice and patience. It is important to accept every measure of progress no matter how small, and to acknowledge any shards of pain that remain.]

Intention: *I am blessing it all.*

Procedure

- In the presence of your compassionate observer, review a painful memory.

- Ask yourself if you are ready to discharge this event, as well as any concept of yourself as a victim of it. If you are, let your memory of the incident stream out of you.

- Forgive all judgments you hold about your participation in the incident, and identify a lesson you may have learned from it.

- Comfort any lingering hurts or fears.

- Visualize yourself planting seeds of loving in the soil of your past. See them taking root in the present and blanketing your future with growth, awareness, and revelation.

Awareness Update

- Record your experience.
    Which piece of your past did you release?
    What inner shifts did you notice while releasing it?
    What lessons did it hold?

Awareness Exercise #5

The laws of fear impose punitive, paralyzing belief systems. When you admit to a fear, come out of hiding, and courageously inch your way forward in the spirit of loving, you begin to encounter a benevolent world where mistakes are allowed and creation insists on happening.

Intention: *I am opening to grace.*

Procedure

- Unmask a fear, either one concealed behind reactions of anxiety or anger, or one numbed over by a compulsive behavior.

- Talk comfortingly to the fear, letting it know that all is well.

- Look for any judgments lurking nearby, and forgive the misunderstandings that gave rise to them.

- Invite the aid of divine assistance.

- Agree to move forward lovingly, to notice "little miracles" that come your way, and to regard them as evidence that you are being supported in your mission.

Awareness Update

- Record your experience.
  What long-denied fear did you uncover?
  What inner shifts did you observe in welcoming divine assistance?

Awareness Exercise #6

COMMITTING FULLY TO SELF-MASTERY

A promise to take responsibility for your human self and develop response-ability toward your divine self is a giant step forward. It ensures vigilance against defaulting to customary beliefs, habitual behaviors, and nonnurturing relationships. Life becomes a perpetual surprise, an adventure in conscious decision-making made manifest through actions.

Intention: *I am choosing to grow.*

Procedure

- Select an aspect of your life that is keeping you joyless and small.

- Examine your story for a limiting belief that might be contributing to the constraints you feel.

- Dismantle the belief and agree to let go of it. Then decide on an action to solidify the larger perception of yourself.

- Review your relationships to see if one or more is prohibiting growth in this area.

- Ask yourself if you are willing to share more authentically in these relationships. Think of an action that would reinforce your liberation from nonnurturing alliances.

- Visualize yourself being true to your essence.

Awareness Update

- Record your experience.
    Which area of your life is not working?
    What new choices did you make?
    How will you fortify these changes?

Awareness Exercise #7

DEEPENING YOUR RELATIONSHIP WITH YOUR DIVINE NATURE

Turning inward from the material bonds of life can be bewildering since nothing discernible in the outer world confirms the existence of sacred inner bonds. And yet heard, felt, or seen experiences of your divine nature may have already clued you in on its presence. Deepening the bonds of this relationship gives way to unending awe, wonder, and mystery.

Intention: *I am partnering with God (Spirit, my divine nature).*

Procedure

- Have a conversation with your divine nature wherever you feel at ease speaking intimately, such as outdoors in nature, over a canvas and set of paints, in the bathtub, or by a roaring fire.

- Let this indwelling source of wisdom know you'd like its help in seeing more clearly and in using your energy more impeccably. Perhaps describe a predicament and ask, "God, what would you do in this situation?" or simply request to be shown what a relationship with God is like.

- Listen closely for guidance, trusting that it may not come immediately or resemble anything you might expect.

- Give your divine nature free reign over an aspect of your life, relinquishing any urge to control this portion of your reality.

- Agree to check in with your divine nature at least once a day, either through prayer, contemplation, meditation, or a spiritual practice. [*Note:* In later stages of this exercise, set an alarm on your watch to go off every two hours, and when it does, remind yourself who's really in charge.]

Awareness Update

✤ Record your experience.

What guidance did you receive?

How did you respond to the contact?

Which aspect of your life did you turn over to God?

PRACTICE

SETTING AN INTENTION TO REMAIN AWARE OF GOD
(SPIRIT, YOUR DIVINE NATURE)

Amidst the rough-and-tumble of daily life, it is easy to lose sight of subtle inner energies. A ready-made intention to remain aware of God can set you back on course. Compose the most relevant intention possible, keep it handy, and use it as a homing device.

- Sit quietly, open your heart, and observe your most immediate experience of God.

- Based on the information you received, create a clear intention to help you remain aware of God. Here are some examples:

    I am hearing the voice of God.

    I am feeling the warmth of my divine nature.

    I am seeing signs of my divinity at work.

    I am at peace inside.

- Concentrate on your intention each time your mind and heart begin looking for a focal point.

- Return to your intention whenever you feel lost in chaos.

- As your contact with God enters another dimension of your experience, create a more customized intention.

Spirit is nearer than your own hands and feet.
You already are what you wish to be.
You are already the divine perfection in your soul. . . .
You are already love. You are already peace.

—JOHN-ROGER[1]

PART IV

Cocreating with
Your Divine Nature

To create is human.
To cocreate is divine—
and that's where heaven making begins.

A HIGHER LEVEL OF COOPERATION

The way into the self is about *me;* the way back out is about *we.* Bringing the light of awareness to the inward-winding trail, the human self suddenly looks over to find a travel companion. It is the divine self, who intimates that it has been present all along. As they dialogue, the human self is treated to two more startling discoveries: creation has been going on all this time, as has cooperation. So on the passage back out, as well as on future escapades in and out, the human self gets to consciously bask in the wisdom and fellowship of the divine self.

The discovery that we are powerful creators unfolds slowly. Eventually we see that we really did create our experience of the past. Because years ago we perceived only a small shiny nugget of ourselves, we stopped showing up for intimacy in important relationships, for exciting career opportunities, voice lessons, whatever seemed to stretch our view of ourselves as anything other than a bantam nugget. In the process, we composed our own experiences of separation, struggle, and suffering. Perhaps you are aware of instances where you unwittingly manufactured deficits out of deficit thinking, or victimhood out of the belief that you were a born victim.

If we have created our experiences thus far, then there is every reason to think we can continue to shape our lives. In partnership with our divine nature, which is already encoded with full knowledge of our potential, we have a chance to cocreate a deeply meaningful reality. All that is needed is the awareness that every moment holds out a splendid opportunity: to either create from our frail and often delusional human nature, or cocreate from the blessed coupling of our human and divine forces. When these two work in tandem, heaven is in the making.

The discovery of cooperation is often more astounding. On hindsight, many people are amazed by the generous assistance they received while cooperating, to whatever extent they could, with their inner guidance. It stands to reason that a higher level of cooperation would yield even greater returns—more of what we need, more of what we want. As it turns out, a high state of cooperation gives us new eyes, and with these we can see what before was invisible.

It is said that while sculpting *David*, Michelangelo chipped away everything that "wasn't David." Something in the slab of marble that was to become David illuminated a form so vividly that with each chisel stroke, the master sculptor was able to bring it to expression. In collaborating closely with our divine nature we, like David, become gently molded and fashioned into who we really are. Some people undergoing this sculpting process feel as if unseen hands are lovingly peeling away defenses that no longer serve them. Others remark that they are no longer preoccupied with the struggle of their soul to extricate itself from beneath a heavy boulder. A fisherman once told me that when he started following the calls of his heart, "barnacles" affixed to him decades before began falling away by the score, and new ones were not attaching as easily. These accounts all end with the mention of new vision.

Engaging in a higher level of cooperation with our divine nature causes us to light up, lighten up, and begin to see ourselves, and in time others, as God sees us—perfect, complete, and good. You can feel this happening each time you choose to expand rather than contract, to love rather than fear, and to forgive rather than condemn. All the while, your divine nature is hard at work, and with every wedge of conditioning it chips away, you come to see this master sculptor and recognize it as your God-self.

Paradoxically, in seeing more you will know less. Statements of certainty ("I know what this experience will be like") will give way to admissions of uncertainty ("I have no idea what this experience will be like"). Ultimately, a high state of cooperation with your divine nature *requires* you to shed the need to know, and simply *be* in the mystery. It's not necessary to know what will happen before you leap, or where the bend in the road leads; you'll find these things out soon enough. Just remain collaborative, loving, responsible, respons-able, and brimming with childlike wonder, for then you will *be* and *see* anew from one enchanted moment to the next.

THE NATURE OF COCREATING

STUDENT: I like the idea of cocreating, but I can't picture it working for me. I'm always messing up and forgetting about my divine nature. Why would it even *want* to collaborate with me?

TEACHER: Because your divine nature knows your full potential and wants to help you express it. As for those lapses in attention, I'd have to say the angels are showing you exactly where to direct your compassion. Each time you focus on these areas, you'll be releasing more self-righteousness and aligning more closely with your divinity.

STUDENT: Are the angels making sure my blunders and failures show up like big dots on the page? Can I look beyond them and see my divinity?

TEACHER: You can if you let down your resistance to cocreation.

STUDENT: Okay, I'll try to warm up to the idea that I really can cocreate. In the meantime, what can I do about my mistakes after looking beyond them? I wish they'd just evaporate.

TEACHER: They will if you deal with them. Any time you make a mess, clean it up—the sooner, the better. Use everything that happens as a vehicle for extending your growth and advancement.

STUDENT: If I deal with the messes, maybe I *would* be a worthy collaborator, or at least a more accountable one.

TEACHER: Yes, and the more accountable you are, the quicker your perspective will shift from blame and punishment toward upliftment.

STUDENT: When I master this shift, will I be able to quickly cocreate opportunities for upliftment rather than endlessly creating opportunities for punishment? Or is *everything* about upliftment, even circumstances that feel punitive?

TEACHER: Now you are becoming your own teacher! Every time you choose to see a situation through the eyes of your divinity, you tap into more of your true nature. See loving and you will manifest loving. See abundance and *that* is what you will manifest. See peace and in that moment you will manifest peace.

STUDENT: Then upliftment really is going on all the time. Therefore, everything that happens in my life is *for* me, not *against* me—even if it sometimes doesn't feel that way.

TEACHER: Always look for the blessing. When you act as if there's a blessing present, you enhance your capacity to perceive blessings.

STUDENT: So if I embrace cocreation, my life can be filled with blessings as long as I bless it.

CHAPTER SIXTEEN

SACRED CONVERSATIONS

Every partnership calls for conversations, and cocreative partner-ships cry out for them daily. Lacking consistent communication with our divinity, it is easy to assume we have been deserted. Why? Because no sooner do we invite Spirit to play a formative role in our lives than our survival tactics stop working. The cause-and-effect "big picture" vanishes. The energy to willfully push forward dissipates. And we begin to think that God has either given up on us or gone on an extended sabbatical.

Sacred conversations remind us that supreme wisdom has in fact altered our course and is very much with us. God, pleased by the offer to conavigate your life, is not about to perch passively in the passenger's seat gazing out at the scenery while you take the same routes as before. Instead, God is behind the wheel, preparing to reveal your magnificence. Your job is to become a faithful con-versationalist, for then you will know not only who is in charge but how to participate responsibly. Conversing with divinity requires proficiency in three tasks: getting on the same wavelength as your spiritual partner, consciously attuning to the transmis-sions, and relaying back messages of your own.

On—and Off—God's Wavelength

I ran into my friend Jan at the neighborhood coffeehouse. She was eager to bring me up-to-date on the turn her life had recently taken. "After fifteen years on the job, I'm no longer selling insurance," she said, almost giddy. "Upon waking up one Monday morning about three months ago, I decided to embark on my dream of training animals to assist the elderly. Although I'd been researching this work sporadically for years, never before did I feel ready to make the leap. That Monday morning I must have been on the same wavelength as the grand architect of my life. Anyway, I'm giving it a go."

"Good for you," I replied. "How's it turning out?"

"You know how I like everything mapped out before I budge? Well, I'm a little nervous because my old radar detector's not telling me what's next. I've got a few clients—referrals from friends—but I have no idea when I'll be earning enough income to pay my bills."

I nodded in recognition. "So your inner architect sent you a message, you were on the right wavelength to receive it, but you can't plot out your month in advance."

"*Month?* I have no idea what *tomorrow* will bring. But I can tell you this is my last leap of faith until I sprout wings. It's hardly the time to lift my feet off the ground."

"So how are you managing without your radar up and running?"

"I'm having to rely on inner guidance all the way. I've developed a little morning ritual: I write down everything that needs to be done in the next twenty-four hours, then I say, *Okay, God, this is what I'm doing today unless you have a better plan. Please assist me in completing my list or tell me where else I need to focus.*"

"Is your collaboration working out?"

"Most days, I proceed as planned and have a sense that I'm on course. But sometimes, I'll get an unexpected phone call about a matter requiring immediate attention and I throw my agenda away. I'm getting good at letting go."

"In spite of the uncertainty, you seem happy," I commented.

"Maybe that's what happens when you begin following a dream that's been in your heart for some time. I feel so fulfilled interacting with the animals. And a part of me is excited about working in tandem with God. Of course, I'm having to check out any message that flies in on that wavelength since it doesn't come with a lot of fanfare." She smiled. "Isn't it just like God to have a poker face!"

While temporarily on the same wavelength as our divinity, we sense that *now* is the time to move forward, or we hear a faint voice telling us to pursue our heart's desire. But at the same time, life as we knew it ceases. The next day refuses to come into focus. Expectations begin bowing to serendipity. Leaving a solid job to gamble on self-employment seems suicidal, yet the heart surges with joy and anticipation. Packing up all earthly possessions and hitting the road becomes more important than figuring out where to live. Declaring an end to "holding back" in intimate discussions could be a set-up for vulnerability, but we heed the call nonetheless.

The divine self encourages these acts of blind trust and faith. But when we slide off its wavelength, as we inevitably do, we return to a human self still attached to old forms of safety and security, and rumbling with caution: *It was another wild card. You're so far out of your comfort zone you'd better keep both feet on the ground.* In response, we may mutter to ourselves, "I thought God came with joy and peace. Well, I don't feel very peaceful."

Transversing these wavelengths as a multidimensional being can take some getting used to. In the early stages, it is helpful to do frequent reality checks, watching for what worked; to put your energy into motion, even if you only take baby steps forward; and to let go of old modes of operation, trusting that assistance will present itself. The postulating of outcomes is not required, though action is. When in doubt, admit to your confusion, saying inside, *I don't know what to do next*—a message that can mobilize the aid of unseen forces. Exercise patience with this new form of intelligence gathering, and every day strive to return to Spirit's wavelength, resuming an earlier conversation or beginning a new one.

Consciously Attuning to God's Transmissions

Divinity is constantly sending instructions, but rarely are they trumpeted forth with ear-splitting bravado or accompanied by diatonic trills. On the contrary, they are conveyed as subtle vibrations traveling at a specific frequency, similar to radio and television transmissions. In random moments, or while dream seeking like Jan, we can instinctively pick up on these currents. But tuning in consciously is a bit more laborious.

First, all "pipelines" to and from the divine must be cleared of obstructions. A pipeline can be anything that serves as a channel for inspiring thoughts, intuitive hunches, body sensations, heart openings, or light "Pay attention" taps on the shoulder. The most common blockages are caused by old beliefs about how divinity shows up (*God appears on mountaintops, not in human beings*), who divinity communicates with (*God doesn't talk to me*), and our capacity to experience a visitation (*I can't hear God*). Once a pipeline is flushed out, it amplifies the volume of incoming messages and excites replies of wonder: *Where did that intuitive flash come from? Why was I directed to this place today? How curious that I would meet up with just the person I was about to call!* or *If I hadn't slowed down, I might have been involved in that accident.*

In addition, to avoid mistaking the dross for the sublime we must learn to distinguish the pitch associated with God's transmissions. Our inner "receiving vessels" are like crystal glasses filled with differing amounts of water; when struck with a soft mallet, each glass vibrates at a certain frequency, producing a pitch of its own. While vibrating in response to a message from Spirit, our receiving vessels produce a pitch that is distinct from all others. Learn to recognize this sound within yourself. The more discerning you can be, the more success you will have in eliminating interference from denser environmental stimuli and in fine-tuning your conversion of Spirit's current into meaningful words. You will know you are calibrating to a message from Spirit if you feel uplifted, encouraged, and supported; never do these transmissions advocate harm to nature's creations.

Finally, to consciously attune to God's transmissions, we must pause, go inside, and shut out the world for a while. Then as we hold an intention to tune in to Spirit, the body's nerve endings stop firing, the mind quiets, the emotions rest, and our awareness expands. With practice, personal retreats in a stress-free setting will automatically open your communication channels to Spirit's flow of direction and sustenance.

Any time safety and security feel threatened during a wild ride with God, there is nothing more refreshing than a daily pause for attunement. A morning prayer, an afternoon river walk, or quiet time in the evening can be enormously fortifying, assuring you that all is well. Fear may be present on some days, but peace will be too. If during a pause you shift your perception from the fear to the peace, braving a quantum leap across multi-dimensional energy bands, safety and security will suddenly take on new meaning.

Relaying Messages to God

Messages from God provide direction and reassurance; messages to God summon what can only be described as illumination. In relaying messages to God, we begin to *see more*—of our truth, our solidarity with Spirit, and our limitless capacity to cocreate a life in which the inconceivable becomes conceivable, and the unmanifest gradually manifest. It's all a matter of holding up our end of sacred conversations.

Imagine that you and your divinity have companion cellular phones. At any time, day or night, you can select a clear channel to God, press the Talk button, and initiate a discussion. You can also reply to incoming signals, thereby keeping the contact alive. So to hold up your end of sacred conversations you need only place outgoing calls and answer incoming ones. God responds well to both efforts.

There are as many opportunities to place a call as there are instances of vulnerability. Inquiries, petitions, and prayers are all welcome. Here are some conversation starters:

When in doubt, ask, *How can I know you more fully?*

In times of overwhelm, ask, *How can I find peace today?*

In moments of fear, say, *Please help me feel your support more deeply right now.*

Amidst confusion, say, *Please show me the highest good in this situation.*

Before a meal, pray, *May this food bring us strength and loving.*

After a disagreement, pray, *May we find our way to a deeper truth.*

In times of fullness, pray, *May my overflow be directed to the upliftment of all.*

God is good at following up on requests for help. But it is unrealistic to expect direct or immediate feedback. An answer may come not from the inner world but from the outer one, in the form of a smile or a surprise visitor. Or it may unfold slowly, requiring inordinate patience on your part. Sometimes patience *is* the solution to a quandary. So after voicing a query, petition, or prayer, pay close attention—inwardly, outwardly, and steadily—for a reply that sheds light on the darkness you are facing.

Responding to God's signals is just as enlightening and often elicits the release of more detailed information. Our feedback can be articulated in countless ways, one of the most effective of which is gratitude. In expressing gratitude for God's loving, our hearts fill with love. In extending appreciation for God's support, our hearts swell with sustenance. All the while, we grow in our capacity to receive.

Ultimately, the offer of openhearted thankfulness for each God-sent message conveys our willingness to be an instrument of Spirit. In turn, we begin to see the blessings hidden behind our disappointments (*That missed promotion must have been a windfall in disguise, because now I can spend more time with my children*), heartaches (*Ending that relationship has shown me what I don't want in the future, and now I can manifest what I do want*), and distress (*It was the most tumultuous year of my life, but now I know what trusting God is all about*).

The most potent response to God's transmissions is to say thank you, hang up the cellular phone, and then act on the message, assuming responsibility for each deed we perform. Through these actions we begin birthing the seed of an idea into physical form. Suddenly we are instruments of Spirit actively participating in the work of creation . . . and the masterpiece we are creating is *ourselves*. We are giving visibility to previously dormant aspects of ourselves, at once expressing more of our potential and manifesting attributes of our divinity.

Sacred conversations till the soil of our heavens. You may wake up one morning and follow an odd prompting to leave your inner safety net and cultivate new turf. As you call upon God for reassurance, comfort streams back, enriching your endeavor with fertilizer. Then more provisions arrive. When you ask for guidance, life-sustaining waters begin to flow. If you express your gratitude, sunlight shines on each furrow you have dug. Moving into action, you plant your first seed and, with ongoing divine assistance, grow the garden of your life.

But this is only the beginning. Other people, seeing the loving and goodness emanating from your little plot of earth, will gather around it. Awed by the abundance of lush vegetation, they may ask a question or two. Some will surely be inspired to realize their own potential, ultimately tilling the soil of more heavens.

YOU CAN MAKE IT HEAVEN

CHAPTER SEVENTEEN

HEAD, HEART, AND HANDS

The real enchantment of cocreation begins when the head, heart, and hands are aligned with divine guidance. The head, seat of intention, holds a clarity of purpose in response to God's message; the heart is open, exuding loving-kindness; the hands are in motion, forming something new, signing on for an endeavor, crafting an idea into a reality. Suddenly it is as if someone turned a spigot and unleashed a flow of formative forces, for we are surging with creative energy. We feel different, a bit lighter and fuller. The world appears more bountiful. The world *is* more bountiful, as people in close proximity will remark.

As miraculous as the cocreative experience feels, all it takes is fine-tuning of the head, heart, and hands in routine moments of everyday life. A little discipline can go a long way. Setting intentions during morning workouts strengthens the mind's capacity to hold a point of focus. Opening the heart with each breath en route to the fax machine hastens the release of loving energy. Quiet acts of service for family members keep divine energy in motion. Finally, short chats with our divine partner while getting into and out of the car heighten our awareness of God's messages.

A slight adjustment here or there, and our world transforms from an obstacle course to a place of deep fulfillment. And unlike most other tasks we tackle, the work of manifestation is energizing yet nonstressful. There's no sweat or frustration, just a realigning of energy pathways so God the Sculptor can reveal more and more of our potential to make a heaven.

Every cocreative partnership hinges on this critical alignment. If we inadvertently forgo intention, sacrifice heart, or forget to take action, the energy comes back at us in the form of a dilemma. If we engage head, heart, and hands, but dismiss our divinity, we can easily create much more than we bargained for—outcomes that make us think, *I'd better be careful what I ask for, because I just might get it.* In either case, the feedback is often immediate and always delivered with tender mercy. Like a skater who has fallen on the ice, we come to our senses, regain our composure, and glide back into the divine flow. With experience, we recover even more quickly and learn that though we may stumble, we can never fall out of the bounds of loving or away from the miracles of cocreation.

A Call to Action

Carol considered herself a born diva. Raised by a doting mother and a father widely celebrated for his musical genius, Carol followed on his coattails, giving her life to the stage. Her talent, intelligence, and exotic demeanor drew large audiences and kept her booked months in advance. The power surging through her on stage let her know early on that God wanted her to sing, so she silently dedicated every performance to Spirit. But one day Carol's forty-year career came to a screeching halt.

Months later, over a mug of steaming coffee, she told me her story. "It was terrifying. My agent was unable to line up a single engagement for me. All those years I'd been showing up on demand—at concert halls, social events, fund-raisers, nightclubs, wherever he'd scheduled an appearance—and suddenly it all ended. I began drifting off to sleep each night thinking God might not love me if I stopped singing."

"What did you do?" I asked, imagining her devastation at having to give up her most precious gift.

Carol took a quick sip of coffee. "First, I asked God to stay close, to lead me through this tunnel of darkness and out the other side. Nothing budged. Then I asked for a burning-bush experience. Still nothing. So for weeks I sat around trying to figure out a new career. I scratched out one scenario after another on paper napkins, complete with pros and cons, do's and don'ts, and numerous 'what ifs.' Worried that God might not be listening, I stayed glued to the kitchen table, rarely leaving the house."

"Did you come up with something viable?"

"Only a stack of useless napkins to throw away, feeling more lost than before. But on impulse one day, I decided to turn in my song sheets for a career in massage therapy. So I drove to a nearby massage school and marched into the registrar's office to enroll. My head was so clogged with Gordian knots that it was a relief to take action. If hands could smile, that's what mine were doing as I signed on the dotted lines."

"So you've retired from the world of entertainment?" I asked, mystified that she would do something so radical.

"Well, I drove home actually trusting that God would accompany me on this new course, one step at a time. It felt so comforting. But no sooner did I set foot in my house than the phone rang. It was my agent, calling to say he'd booked me at a club in New York—one I'd been wanting to sing at for ages!"

"Then you're back on stage?"

"Yes, and busier than ever. I'm even recording a CD."

"What do you suppose Spirit was trying to tell you all that time?"

"Two things," Carol said, diving back into her mug, a glimmer in her eyes. "One was that I didn't have to sing to receive God's love—which by the way never did erupt in flames. The other lesson was about cocreating: it seems that stewing over napkins creates nothing but stew. Only when I took action did my energy start moving, as if God were cheering me on."

Carol's story shows how easy it is to feel shaken in this stage of cocreation and to disrupt the flow of precious energy. If you, like Carol, find large chunks of personal identity falling away during the sculpting process, try not to become overly absorbed in figuring out what to do next. The head, on its own, is ill equipped to determine outcomes, much less shape them. Thoughts working overtime may only draw in feelings of despair. When all you can see in the outer world is chaos breaking loose, trust the inner voice that says "all is well," redirect your mind to an intention, keep your heart open to loving, and *take action*.

If your mind has already become embroiled in a loss of identity, remember that a new piece of yourself is coming to expression. Step back into the ineffable movement of cocreation and you will soon come out the other side being more of who you really are. This can only happen with your active cooperation.

A call to action is purposeful *whether or not we know where we are going*. It ushers us solidly into the current of change. Invariably we falter in our most broken, fragile, or guarded places—and that is where God swoops us up for cocreation.

A Bid for Openheartedness

I first met Dan ten years ago while volunteering at a community event for the homeless. He was a well-respected philosophy professor planning to dedicate his life to God. Right away I noticed his intensity, his piercing eyes, and the crease running up the center of his forehead. He relaxed a bit as we spent a few moments bantering over interpretations of religious scripture, most of which he could recite verbatim.

Recently we met quite by chance at an outdoor market, but this was a different Dan entirely. His gaze, softer now, shimmered with serenity; his energy seemed boundless, joyful; and he radiated an aura of peace.

"My goodness, you're looking sublime," I commented. "Did God just take you out for lunch?"

"No free lunches with the Creator," he said, laughing. "But you're right, I'm feeling a lot fuller these days."

"You weren't exactly running on 'empty' last we met," I quipped. "You seemed to be walking and talking with the Master Refueler himself."

"It might have looked that way," Dan replied, "but I was actually a self-righteous, driven, obsessive madman going through the motions of how I thought a spiritual person would act—like some windup apostle. My devotion was not to God but to an image of God I'd constructed in my head."

"When did you come to *that* realization?" I asked, startled that his earlier fervor had been sparked by a concept of union rather than an authentic experience of it.

"Well, about five years ago I began to gamble. Every once in a while I'd take a few dollars and head out to a casino for a night of innocent fun. But before long I was a 'regular.' I'd immerse myself in piety by day and decadence at night, a paragon of greed, lust, and addiction. I was petrified, ashamed—knee-deep in a crisis of faith. I didn't want God to find me there. If he does, I told myself, he will cross me off the honor roll and most likely expel me from his ivy-strewn tower."

"Is that what happened?" I wanted to know.

"Actually, God *dissembled* the tower, and it was not his at all—it had loomed sky-high in my own mind. Here's what happened: At the blackjack table one night, my mind gave up its turmoil and my heart opened. I prayed silently, *I don't know if you can hear me from this hellish abyss, God, but I need help. I cannot make peace with my degradation. Have you given up on me? How can I find my way back into your grace?* God answered by flooding me with love. Meeting God in this ungodlike place blew off any latches that remained along the edges of my heart. And I knew firsthand that God is in everything—the frailty and the strength, the earth and the sky, night and day. Recognizing that God was even in my addiction, I stopped hiding and lightened up."

"Have you given up gaming?" I asked.

"I've given up all my games—the gambling, the rhetoric, the arrogance, the swarm of community events each week, and others. Now when I'm engrossed in conversations about a religious text, there's another party in attendance: my heart. As a result, I am able to perceive a divine presence and, odd as this may sound, the words of scripture spring to life. Plus, having my heart on the scene keeps me humble. Those are good odds."

The heart, source of real abundance and true wisdom, provides the cohesion needed for cocreation. Whereas the mind tends to segment information into opposing categories of thought, the heart can fuse them back together into a seamless whole. For example, thought alone may have us perceiving vulnerability as a weakness and invulnerability as a strength—a notion that can only polarize the flow of energy moving toward cocreation. But after adding heart to the equation, we are able to see that there is vulnerability in our strength and strength in our vulnerability. When this notion is aligned with our actions and divine guidance, the inconceivable can easily take form.

Any time you feel the need to open your heart a little more, remind yourself that God is no prima donna. Your divinity would never insist on four-star accommodations featuring good moods and elevated spirits. You can be in a pit of despair asking for signs of God's presence and your prayer will be answered, whereupon your heart will expand even more. To keep it open wide, bring your loving everywhere—to your thoughts, your words, and your actions. Love your foibles. Embrace your all-too-human frailties. Caress the walls of your darkest hideouts. Loving is a passport to enlightenment.

The Manna of Cocreation

Several of us had gathered for Passover to commemorate the Israelites' freedom from slavery in Egypt. Phil opened the Seder service by reading from the Hebrew text. I was three seats away, transported by the rhythm and timbre of his voice. It was as if I were among the Israelites fleeing with Moses through the wilderness of Sinai 3,400 years ago. The heat was intense. The mood, determined. When I brought myself back to the service, God's power was everywhere—in the flickering of the candle flame, the bitter herbs on the Seder plate, the pile of matzo symbolizing the manna supplied to the pilgrims during their exodus, and in the air itself.

Later lingering at the buffet table, I caught up with Phil. "The Passover prayers seemed to rise up in you from a place of perpetual relationship with the divine. How does this happen?" I asked.

He connected inwardly before answering. "One of the blessed mysteries of life is that God ushers us out of captivity and into creativity. But if we forget about God, it is easy to retract into a state of bondage."

"Have you experienced bondage in your own life?" I asked, wondering how he could speak so assertively about the sense of spiritual abandonment.

"Umm," he said, stroking his trim white beard. "For most of my life I was running fear so much that I eventually named it Mr. Trouble—Mr. T., for short." He smiled, his eyes twinkling. "Whenever Mr. T. was up and about, I felt apprehensive around people. If I wasn't jealous of someone's accomplishments or envious of their relationships, I was suspicious of their motives for being with me. My fear was probably about failing at anything I do."

"And it kept you enslaved, separating you from God?"

"It did until about three months ago when I began working with Mr. T. through a Tibetan practice of inhaling God with every breath and directing it to the scared place inside me. Acknowledging my fear instead of avoiding it, has since become a spiritual practice. But breathing God into my fear transformed my universe, inside and out."

"I daresay the outside part is apparent. It awakened some latent power in me to travel swiftly across time and space. But what's it like on the inside?"

"There's an unexpected warmth that tells me I'm okay and all is well. I am filled with a new sense of freedom," Phil crooned. "I'm seeing more vividly, too. It's like pulling out of the car wash with a clean windshield: everything's brighter and more colorful. The world I see now is permeated with love."

"It sounds like you're not so reactive around people anymore," I commented.

"Actually I relish the manna in simple interactions. I see God as clearly in smiles of happiness as in brows furrowed with weariness, as radiantly in the clasped fingers of lovers as in the courtly hands of diplomats. So I've revised my definition of success: it's about staying in touch with that magnificence. And sure enough, I'm never separated from divine love. I'm convinced that none of us is, but every now and then it's a good idea to hose down the windshield."

Phil's head, heart, and hands were so perfectly aligned with his divinity that in our brief time together he had manifested freedom. The cause of his fear mattered little, for it had been diluted and transformed by infusions of love. Now Phil and his divinity were one and the same—a source of divine nourishment. And there was nothing he had to *do* other than make the choice to *be*. That is the secret formula for heaven building.

Ultimately cocreation leads to the discovery that there are no problems to tackle, just opportunities for being. Any time you think there *is* a problem, try lifting the veil inside that might be separating you from your true nature; then come back to *be*ing. For Phil, that veil was fear. For others, it can be worry or anxiety.

Whenever you feel yourself reacting to an external event—whether out of fear, worry, or anxiety—lift the veil of preconception and see what happens. You may hear God saying, "Okay, Beloved, here's the bondage we'll break free of today." Or perhaps God will step right in, permeating the darkness with light. Whether bidden or unbidden, your cocreative partner is sure to show up with provisions for emancipation and sustenance. You need only be grateful.

It is in being that we recognize just how extraordinary the ordinary is. In being we also realize that the next moment will usher in an unmanifested heaven. Illumined and at liberty to be fully ourselves, no matter how mundane, we can manifest that heaven.

CHAPTER EIGHTEEN

MANIFESTING A HEAVEN OR TWO

Manifesting is like birthing. It's a means of giving visibility to an inner reality, bringing it forth into the world. In birthing a baby, we allow the fullness of a gestating human being to emerge into a life of its own, no longer confined to a womb or tethered to an umbilical cord. Manifesting a heaven is much the same: an overflow of cocreative forces spills outward into expression. Both processes empty us for ongoing growth, expansion, and revelation, now sparked from the outside.

Heavens are like babies in another respect too: while they're still in utero, we have a sense of their most salient features. So if you have been consciously cocreating, you are probably aware of the new qualities and attributes welling up within you and yearning for visibility. Perhaps these spring from the energy of abundance, loving, joy, or the forces of freedom, vibrant health, compassion, or peace.

The kaleidoscopic dance of cocreation igniting these new levels of energy may even be spilling over into your interactions with others. Many people engaged in cocreation are surprised at how lighthearted they feel in previously troublesome situations, suddenly responding to a boss's demands with easygoing cooperation, to a child's temper tantrums with eyes of compassion, or to a querulous neighbor with offerings of peace. There is no expectation of return, for these are simply embryonic outpourings of a heaven stretching and growing within.

Once aware that you are incubating a rapidly enlarging heaven on the inside, there is much you can do on the outside to make way for the birth. You can prepare a spacious nesting place by clearing out closets, the garage, the basement, and any piles of clutter congregating in your bedroom. Pay special attention to your health as well, making sure you get fresh air, exercise, wholesome nutrition, and plenty of sleep. Also greet each day with wonder and anticipation, immerse yourself in nature as often as possible, and note any perceptions of quickening inside. An attitude of buoyant receptivity softens borders between the inner and outer worlds.

Although heavens are never premature or in need of immediate resuscitation, they are precious and worthy of the best passage possible. To minimize any likelihood of complications, enlist the services of God as your leading midwife. Then prepare a birth plan to submit to God, participate actively in the manifestation, and as time passes, share your heaven with the world.

A First-Rate Birth Plan

A comprehensive birth plan for most any heaven has two components: an intention and a clear picture of the new heaven in action. Both these elements can be recorded on a sheet of paper and submitted to God, at which point the manifestation begins.

The intention. A birth practitioner wants to know where the delivery is to take place—at home, in a birthing center, or at the hospital—and God is no exception. Your divine midwife needs to be told exactly where in your life you would like your heaven manifested.

To identify this part of your intention, reflect on your day-to-day reality: Where is the hell you would most like to transform? You might tell yourself, "I'd sure like my finances to reflect this surge of abundance," or "My relationships could definitely use an infusion of this loving," or "It's time to have some of this joy at my workplace."

As soon as you have decided where you would like your heaven manifested, set your intention with that it mind. Because your energy will follow this intention, be sure to keep it defined and directed. If you want your inner sense of abundance to flow into your financial affairs, you might write: *I am cocreating my perception of finances to manifest my inner abundance, the fullness that is me.* If you'd like your loving to spill over into your relationships, you could write: *I am cocreating my view of relationships to manifest the loving within me.* For joy at work, your intention might be: *I am cocreating my vision of work to manifest the joy that flows inside me.*

The picture. This portion of the birth plan lets your divine midwife know exactly how you see the heaven manifesting. As its energy becomes visible, what changes will it foster in your life? Using creative imagination and expansive ideas, put pen to paper, but only after exploring the following questions:

⤸ How might your finances, relationships, or workplace begin to reflect your inner fullness?

> In terms of finances, can you see yourself reducing debt and building up savings? Do you envision increasing your productivity and client base? Can you imagine generating an income that enhances your quality of life and that of others?

> With regard to relationships, can you see yourself releasing past disappointments and welcoming fulfillment? Do you envision being more demonstrative? Can you imagine expressing a depth of caring that encourages others to be exactly who they are?

> As for work, can you see yourself becoming more authentic at your place of employment? Do you envi-

sion permeating your workday with more humor and gratitude? Can you imagine exuding a vitality that uplifts your coworkers?

❧ What beliefs or perceptions stand in the way of a more expansive relationship with money, other people, or work?

Concerning finances, do you believe debt is bad? Do you assume it is difficult to hold on to money? Do you suspect that you don't have what it takes to generate wealth?

Regarding relationships, do you believe people cannot be trusted? Do you assume you lack the capacity to love and be loved? Do you see a necessity for controlling others to avoid getting hurt?

With respect to business, do you associate work with drudgery? Do you believe it's unprofessional to show delight and pleasure on the job? Do you see yourself as lacking in skills, talent, or luck?

❧ In what facet of financial management, relationship dynamics, or workplace perspectives could you commit to growing?

In dealing with finances, could you further develop your stewardship of money? Might you invest in a perception of money as energy? Would you consider expanding your capacity to receive?

In relationships, could you show more compassion to yourself and others? Might you cultivate kindheartedness as your first response? Would you consider listening more deeply during conversations?

At work, could you liberate more of your spontaneity and authenticity? Might you strive for making a difference? Would you consider elevating your bottom line to encompass more of your valued truths?

As much as possible, adapt these birth plan guidelines to your individual desires. Your preferred birth setting may be unrelated to the financial, relationship, or workplace domain; it could be child rearing, for example, or eldercare, home beautification or gardening, a dormant talent or fascination, or a hobby, sport, or artistic endeavor. Wherever you would like your heaven to emerge, state it succinctly in your intention and picture it clearly. The same holds true for the new energy arising within you; instead of abundance, loving, or joy, it might be freedom or vibrant health, compassion or peace. However you experience the energy of your heaven-to-be, identify it in your intention and use it to envision your picture.

Once your birth plan is complete, release it to God with a prayer asking for this heaven or an even better one. Simultaneously, let go of any attachment to your picture of heaven in action. Strive for your stated ideals but prepare for anything, aware that divine assistance is intent on bringing about *the greatest good for all concerned*—something we ourselves cannot possibly know. Even our own greatest good is beyond our understanding.

Remember that God, although eager to know your objectives, does not operate a wish fulfillment service geared toward manifesting particular dollar amounts in a bank account, entertainment venues for a budding relationship, or on-the-job travel opportunities. Rather, God's purpose is to serve you in the most growth-promoting way possible.

Manifestation

Whereas most human babies are born within hours of the first birth pangs, heavenly infants can take weeks, months, or sometimes years to fully manifest. This passage is rich with transformation. Day by day, tangible signs of the emergence can come into view. For example, you may notice a dramatic turn for the best in health or proficiency, long-locked doors suddenly opening to you, or people being unusually cooperative with you. One woman I know saw her compassion manifesting when, during a near crisis with her beloved dog, instead of being swept away by panic she instinctively opened her heart and supervised a rescue mission with gentle strength, remaining a calm in the center of her storm.

The sustained momentum of manifestation requires your active collaboration. To support the work of your divine midwife, be sure to affirm your intention at least once a day, and more often in times of chaos. Confusion, once imbued with sacred intention, will rapidly disperse. In addition to affirming your intention, express gratitude to your divinity each time another chunk of heaven comes forward. Your thankfulness for this miracle can hasten its emergence.

Also focus daily on your picture of heaven, but don't get attached to the particulars. Attachment to details can cause expectations, disappointments, and needless suffering, especially while in the throes of a momentous transition such as heaven making. Any time you are beset by nagging goals or timelines, turn your attention instead to the loving presence of the midwife guiding your manifestation.

Further support comes with ongoing efforts at cocreation. Converting divine energy into the formation of an outer heaven through the alignment of head, heart, and hands is comparable to the work of a woman in labor; even slight adjustments can ease the baby's passage through the birth canal. So remain mindful of the forces overflowing from inside, keep your heart warm with loving-kindness, and make sure your hands stay active, massaging spirit into matter as if bringing down the stars.

Because your time and energy are at a premium during manifestation, also be sure to conserve these commodities. One way to conserve time and energy is by simplifying your life. Another way is by making decisions that are true to your innermost self, improvising when necessary. A third way to practice conservation is by taking time with yourself on a regular basis, even if only for a cup of tea; a little solitude can go a long way. Keeping company with yourself may prove to be your most effective means of reconnecting with your birthing companion, acknowledging your own life-giving forces, and confirming your well-being. At the very least, it is apt to help you approach your waking hours more softly and still accomplish the day's missions.

A final supportive measure in times of manifestation is to conduct your life as if it were a living prayer. Revise the details of your sacred picture whenever necessary. Also remember your priorities, remain faithful to them, and after slipping up, practice forgiveness. If it turns out that you have lost your bearings, get back on track through realignment. If you have encountered a mental or emotional block, clear the obstruction through self-mastery. If limiting beliefs have been parading through your mind, disentangle yourself from them. Liberate yourself from everything that is not of your essence, pray to your Master Sculptor, and carry on with the business of manifesting until your heaven has fully emerged. As French aviator and novelist Antoine de Saint-Exupéry poignantly wrote, "You know you have achieved perfection in design not when you have nothing more to add, but when you have nothing more to take away."

Following the birth of your first heaven, you will be more knowledgeable in the nuances of manifestation. A greater part of you will be available to deliver another heaven. Best of all, you'll be able to step forward and claim your birthright as a powerfully abundant and loving cocreator.

Sharing Heaven with the World

Imagine a world in which relationships were woven of heavens instead of hells, in which families supported authenticity and diversity among their members, schools rewarded intuitive insights and fresh ideas, businesses granted compassion awards, and communities celebrated openheartedness. Imagine a planet of people so committed to inner growth and expansiveness that no one would be allowed to go hungry, homeless, or without medical care . . . so devoted to honoring everyone's divine nature that oppression and exploitation would be unthinkable . . . so dedicated to fostering peace and plenty that more than 130 species of trees per hectare would grace formerly logged-over forests, as is true in the Dayak tembawangs of western Borneo, and bountiful wildlife populations would flourish in previously damaged native habitats, as they do in California's Channel Islands. Such notions are not far-fetched once we have experienced a heaven gently streaming from us, transforming everyday life from a tangled maze to a place so rich with flow that nothing can stop its course.

Heavens, like toddlers, are rarely content to stay in their own backyards. Unlike toddlers, though, they can be in many places at once, working their magic simultaneously in others' lives and our own. Every heaven has a way of doing this. If you have manifested freedom, as Phil did at the Seder, the energy of freedom will ripple outward toward others, touching the divine freedom at their core—and you will still be blessed with freedom. If you have manifested vibrant health, compassion, or peace, *that* is what will flow into the world. The same holds true for abundance, loving, and joy. Heavens never decrease by being shared. On the contrary, they become nourished that much more. For example, there's nothing so joyous as being a messenger of joy.

When each of your heavens is ready to leave home, you get to direct its course. This kind of guidance is the work not only of a manifester but of a world citizen consciously serving as the head, heart, and hands of divinity. While God continues to infuse your heaven with energy, you have the chance to choose where it will go and how it might get there.

As a world citizen fully aware of how much you are loved and provided for, you can begin searching your heart for ways to enrich the lives of others so that they too might flourish. To share heavenly abundance, you might decide to sponsor a fund-raiser for a student whose family cannot afford college tuition, to donate goods or services toward promoting awareness of your local eco-system, tithe a portion of your income to food for the hungry or clothing for the poor, or provide a home for people with AIDS. To extend a heaven of loving, you could become a foster parent, mentor a teenager, take part in grassroots political reform, be the calm in the center of someone else's storm, turn a heart from fear to love, pray daily for people in strife, foster goodwill overseas, or help clean up the environment. To spread blessings of joy, you might smile often and laugh out loud, bring happiness to children in crisis, refresh and adorn the home of someone in distress, post a Web site to disseminate innovative ideas for social reform, or be a delighted guardian of nature. Or perhaps you will bestow your special gift as a kind-hearted freedom fighter, a beacon of health, a bearer of compassion, an architect of peace, or an angel-in-disguise prompting others to explore their essence.

Having tasted the sweetness of a heaven, we cannot help but offer it to others. People with stage fright share these blessings quietly; extroverts are more vocal, often promoting a cause. Some individuals devise incremental strategies for changing a little corner of the world, whereas others improvise as they go. All offerings born of blessings are blessings.

Heaven sharing, no matter how it unfolds, reveals what we have been searching for all along: our essence, our magnificence, the ability to improve our life circumstances and help build a better world. As the French novelist Marcel Proust so wisely observed, "The voyage of discovery lies not in finding new landscapes but in having new eyes." These are eyes that see beyond illusions forged by a limited understanding of who we are, eyes that see behind the dots of our lives, eyes that see as God sees.

PRACTICE

Bringing Forth a Heaven

A long walk with Spirit takes us from glimpsing a heaven within (see the practice on pages 34–35) to consciously cocreating it to finally bringing it forth. Manifesting a heaven is a sacred act of birthing. As such, it calls for complete immersion in the web of life that flows from invisibility to visibility. With the following guidelines in place, you can easily enter this flow to enrich your existence and propagate more fullness in the world.

- Prepare a birth plan that includes an *intention* stating where you would like to manifest your fullness and a *picture* of how you envision it functioning in your life.

- Turn your birth plan over to God, asking for this heaven or a more enriching one.

- Work cocreatively—keeping your head, heart, and hands aligned with divine guidance—all the while living prayerfully and focusing daily on your intention.

- Each time your fullness overflows into visibility, offer gratitude. When your heaven has completely emerged, embrace it and nourish it with love.

- Once you have fully integrated the spirit-filled reality into your daily life, choose an additional recipient for it—a person, a community of people, or an aspect of planetary life—and begin serving as a conduit for this flow.

- Celebrate your heaven, have fun with it, and others will too.

PART V

Seven Keys to Make Your Life a Heaven

Heaven is an inside job. Your 'heaven' asks you:
What do you truly want? What will give your
life meaning, purpose and fulfillment?

HOW TO USE THE 7 KEYS TO MAKE YOUR LIFE A HEAVEN

These 7 keys are highlighted here in the second edition of Heaven to assist you in focusing on a key or two that could help you at this time to explore deeper.

Choosing to live your life as a heaven – that is, dedicating the inner time and commitment to shift major limiting beliefs in your life – is a radical choice. But the radicalness of that choice can make all the difference.

Use this section to reflect and to consider where you would like to begin. Perhaps you know that you need to begin making different (better) choices for yourself. Or you want to stop your habitual, negative self-talk and learn to love all parts of you. Maybe you are seeking a true connection to your Divine Nature so you can know yourself in truth.

Whatever key you decide to use to begin unlocking your heaven is the right key for you. And you can begin anywhere. For Spirit knows your heart and what you are seeking.

Although there are resources at the end of this 7 Keys section, this is not a "how-to," step-by-step outline to mastering these keys. That is a process that, honestly, cannot be written down. It must be experienced. And it must be experienced in a well-crafted course or school that knows how to walk you through the experiences necessary to go beyond choosing a key to mastering a key.

If you are interested in the "how-to," I encourage you to consider the Heaven on Earth Wisdom School One – Self-Mastery:

Building Your Wisdom Bridge, which you will find on my Sacred Wisdom Teachings Membership site (www.RebeccaESkeele.com/ membership). Go to the Mastery area.

Also, if you purchased the "Keys to Make My Life a Heaven Journal," you will have a handy place to keep your notes, your thoughts, and your insights as your "heaven" comes into view.

As you choose to take the radical journey of discovering and living your heaven on earth, your life will transform in every way. Many blessings to you for your choice and for the path ahead.

In the loving,
Rebecca

ENVISION AND DESCRIBE
YOUR HEAVEN

If you were to live your life as a heaven, what would that look like?

The exercise on page 34 was introduced at the end of Section One, but now let's take it a bit further. I also want to add the following comments.

Sometimes when we are beginning to glimpse a greater life of abundance and loving, what becomes very clear is what our "heaven" is not. You can know what you don't want before you know what you do want. And that's a good process to go through in getting to your inner heaven.

So perhaps start there. When are you not in your heaven? After reading the book, I'm sure you would agree that if you are in a shame-hole or judging yourself harshly, you are not in your heaven – rather, you are in your inner "hell." Also, if you are running the past on the present and dredging up old hurts and wounds – you are not in your heaven.

I have discovered it is important to realize when I have created, promoted, or allowed an experience of my inner "hell." Usually I experience my "hell" when I dwell on past hurts or past disappointments. This realization can assist me to turn toward my inner heaven and make a different choice.

Some days my inner heaven is simply feeling relief that I spent time with myself and cleared my negativity by using acceptance and forgiveness. I then watch my thoughts and feelings carefully so I don't re-engage with what I just cleared.

Other days my heaven is a state of quiet and calm, enabling me to do what I know is on purpose for me in my life.

Because I do have a present and alive spiritual practice, my daily meditations and prayer time are also part of my heaven. In fact, doing my daily spiritual practice makes it easier for me to notice when I slip into a hellish place inside; this assists me to open my heart with compassion to myself and do what I need to do to balance myself.

Here is the exercise from the end of Section One. If you have not done this exercise for yourself, you may want to begin here to discover your inner heaven. If you have already envisioned your heaven, you may want to review and update. Heavens can expand at any time.

* * *

Most notions of heaven refer to the afterlife. Here, however, you will concentrate on this life, capturing impressions left by special objects you have seen or images portrayed in books, movies, or paintings; discarding those you have outgrown; and inviting input from your inner teacher. Clearing out the old makes way for the new.

PART I

✂ Across the top of a sheet of paper, write, "Heaven is . . ." Complete and repeat this phrase as many times as you wish, jotting down images that flash through your mind. Include as much detail as possible.

✂ Next, think deeply about each image, then delete those that are no longer relevant. For example, if you described heaven as a place with puffy white clouds at the top of a long staircase reserved for dead football players—as in the film Heaven Can Wait—but you do not currently envision heaven with puffy white clouds and football players, delete this item.

✂ Finally, beside each remaining item, note the feelings it evokes within you. For instance, if you wrote, "Heaven is a shiny red sports car," describe what it would be like to drive this car. If you wrote, "Heaven is a mutually loving, supportive partnership," describe how you would feel in this relationship.

PART II

✂ Take a deep breath, close your eyes, and ask your inner teacher, "What is heaven?"

✂ Next, imagine that you are facing a large movie screen. Continuing to breathe deeply and calmly, allow whatever images arise to slowly appear on the screen. Make a mental note of your experience before opening your eyes.

✂ Finally, on a second sheet of paper, draw this new glimpse of heaven or portray it in words or symbols.

✂ Write today's date on both sheets of paper and file them for safekeeping.

KEY 2

YOU DON'T NEED FIXING – YOU NEED LOVING

In my spiritual counseling practice, time after time, people would come into my office, sit down, and tell me their pain or their hurt or describe the chaos in their life. After giving them time to share, invariably they would say something like: *I'm sure it has every-thing to do with me. Something must be wrong with me. So please fix me.*

I heard this a lot.

When I started my own healing journey years ago, I thought I needed fixing as well. *There must be something wrong with me. That's why my marriage ended. That's why my teenage kids are acting out. That's why I still feel this way even though it happened 20 years ago. That's why I'm depressed. That's why my life is a mess. That's why I never get ahead. That's why I'm not enough X, Y, Z. In other words, it's something to do with me, and I need to be fixed.*

What if there's really nothing wrong with you?

Your feelings are not wrong; your thoughts are not wrong;

even what happened was not wrong. However, to shift your feelings and thoughts you must commit to making a change. And the change has to do with learning how to work inside yourself with loving, compassion, and acceptance; you must set forth on a path to self-love.

This journey to learn to love all the parts of you can be painful, scary, confusing, challenging, fascinating, and beautiful. In Heaven you read several stories about how people from all walks of life discovered that by loving parts that were hurting or angry or in despair and shame, they actually created more loving in their life – and consequently more happiness.

And they also discovered that there was nothing to be fixed.

If this is the Key for you, where could you bring more loving to yourself? And how can you begin to let go of the limiting belief that you need to be fixed?

What if you are 100 percent perfect just the way you are?

WAKE UP FROM THE KNOCK ON THE DOOR

You know, life is full of knocks. Some of them are pretty gentle and don't require a lot of introspection. For instance, maybe you go to the doctor and she says, *You're cholesterol is a little high. I'd like you to change your diet.* And you say, *Yes, okay, got it. I'll do that.*

Or she says, *It would be good if you lost some weight and go on an exercise program.* You agree: *Yeah, that would be good, too. And you do that.*

Or maybe a boss calls you into her office and she says, *You know, you're doing a great job in this area, but over here I'd really like more attention. I'd like you to up your game over here.* And you agree. *Sure. I'll be glad to do that.*

Or maybe you have a conversation with a good friend and they share with you some behavior lately that has hurt their feelings. You were unaware. So you say, *Thank you. I had no idea that you were affected in that way. I will take a look at that.*

These examples are gentle knocks. They do wake us up. They wake us out of some kind of unconscious pattern or out of an area we were not really aware of. They can bring greater awareness to us.

But what about the knocks in your life that require a life evaluation? I call these the *2x4s of life*. As I mentioned in Chapter Two, the 2x4s usually come out of the blue, and they can shatter a life. You wonder: *Why did this happen? I didn't want this!* And you can feel like victim. The knee-jerk reaction is to try and fix it and put your life back the way it was.

Yes, internal pain can accompany the major 2x4s of life. You can be shocked and experience disappointment. It's not something that you necessarily relish walking through. I know by the time I was 35 years old, I had had a series of these 2x4s, and my life was in pieces all over the floor. Everything that I had thought my life was supposed to be about—everything that I thought I was supposed to be about—felt like a big illusion. I woke up, and I woke up very soberly, and said to myself: *Okay, I have no idea what's next.* What I didn't know at the time was I was being shaken so I could wake up out of a "sleep" and discover my truth. The truth of me.

Is there an area of your life that you are sleepwalking through? Do you know, if you are honest with yourself, that this area needs to shift, to change?

Is it time for you to take that deeper journey? That journey that feels way out of your comfort zone?

As I describe in *Heaven*:

The 2x4s are great awakeners. They are capable of catalyzing unparalleled insights on initial impact. They can easily hurl you back into sleep. For you may be too fraught with pain or fear or resentment or anger or upset to find any value in them. And that is a choice.

It takes considerable courage to go beyond the hurt of a trauma. But timing doesn't matter. What counts is waking up to answer the greater call. Then you begin to transform your life.

KEY 4

GET TO KNOW YOUR TRUE SELF

If I were to ask you to describe yourself, what would you say?

Would you say you are a good person? Loyal? Kind and considerate? Would you describe your roles: mother, father, friend, family member, job title? And would you also know the masks you wear? The ways you show up in different areas of your life to gain approval or recognition?

I call these masks *copies* – facsimiles of what is true about you.

Why? Because the truth of who you are is not the roles you play or the faces you present to the world. The truth of you is beyond all of that.

Here is a quote from Jo Coudert that begins Chapter One of *Heaven*:

It is rewarding to find someone who you know and like, but it is essential to like yourself. It is quickening to recognize that someone is a good, decent human being, but it is indispensable to view yourself as acceptable. Oh, it is a delight to discover people who are worthy of respect and admiration and love, but it is vital to believe yourself deserving of these things.

For you cannot live in someone else. You cannot find yourself in someone else. You cannot be given a life by someone else. Of all the people you will know in a lifetime, you're the only one you will never leave nor lose. To the question of your life you're the only answer. To the problems of your life, you are the only solution.

To discover the true-ness of you and to like and love yourself takes a deeper exploration beyond all of the "clutter" that has masked your bright light. The clutter I am referring to is your judgments about your life; your behavior you deem as less than acceptable; your emotions that can run from A to Z; your feelings of being separate and alone. Do you feel connected and belonging? OK or not OK? And then there is all the judgments you have about others and how you protect yourself from the "other."

You might ask yourself, well, how do I get beyond all of that? Yes, the task can seem daunting; so start simply.

The first step is awareness. And awareness comes from observing your thoughts, your feelings, and your knee-jerk reactions. What begins to emerge after practicing Observation and other Self-Mastery skills is the truth of you – or what is called your *True Self*. Your True Self is not your ego, not the masks you put on to impress, and not the roles you play in your life.

It is the deeper truth, and that truth includes that you are completely 100 percent deserving of loving, of praise, of admiration, of acceptance, of health, of wealth, of happiness, and all the other delightful experiences at the banquet table of life.

KEY 5

CREATE A SAFE PLACE WITHIN

Of all of the self-mastery tools that I teach in the Heaven on Earth Wisdom School, creating a safe place within is probably the most profound. And I would say it's the biggest life-shifting tool that, when applied, creates the most opening beyond the mental and emotional clutter.

How do you create a safe place within? By opening your heart to yourself and extending compassion to those parts of you that are in pain, that feel lost or overwhelmed, that have been shamed or blamed in the past and that feel like they don't fit in or belong.

The safe place within becomes an internal space for all of those parts to be able to come and express themselves without judgment – without being told: *That's not OK. You cannot say that here.* It's an experience of feeling loved and accepted, even if that part is angry, sad, feeling separate and alone, or afraid of ridicule or abandonment.

Many times we want others to hear us, to acknowledge our feelings. Important? Yes. But not as important as learning to listen and acknowledge our own inner feelings and thoughts. You must first learn to do that for yourself. To be heard with compassion means that you do not judge or ridicule yourself. You do not see a part of you as needing to be banished or wiped out. When you can allow all parts to come forward and you are just be "with" those parts – they feel safe. And consequently, you feel safe with yourself.

How can you experience safety and trust with others if you do not first have that within you?

When you decide to create a safe place within, the "light" that you carry can shine into the dark corners where you have relegated "bad" memories, "wrong" behavior, or old shame and blame. That light is your compassion. When you know and practice this self-mastery tool, there is no more need for self-protection, fear, or denial.

And the results from practicing this key is calm, peace, and less stress and tension. It results in loving—an experience of loving that is beyond the common, transient loving that we turn on or off like a water fountain. This loving is who you are. And this loving is eternal.

KEY 6

UNMASK FEAR

The common masks of fear are: anger, anxiety, depression, distraction, control, addiction, and denial. Why do we mask fear? Because to unmask fear leaves us with a feeling of vulnerability, of being unprotected and not safe.

This approach makes sense to our human nature. But you are more than your human nature. What if that unrecognized fear is really masking an unclaimed personal power? And what if you unmasked it – and allowed yourself to explore the fear further— would you discover a greater ability of *you* that could make all the difference in your life?

Is there a cost in staying distracted and avoiding the fear?

Yes. Because the fear is controlling you. It's controlling your life. It's stopping you from really living the life you envision. It can keep you stuck in a dead-end job, an abusive relationship, or a situation that is not serving you in any way. And fear can create all manner of internal, negative self-talk and limiting beliefs.

The opportunity to address fear in your life is to see fear as a messenger. And a messenger has a message. What is the message?

If you approach the fear in a compassionate way, you will find that the message is always showing you an aspect of you that is ready to be claimed in a positive way. You can, through learning to work with yourself with loving, turn that feeling of "danger – fear is present" into expansion and self-acceptance.

And when you transform that fear, your heaven begins to present itself.

MAKE NEW CHOICES

Can you make a different choice, right now, about a situation or circumstance? Or do you feel like a victim to this situation and don't see you have a choice? Is the change coming from outside, and you didn't ask for it nor want it?

A key to *making your life a heaven* is realizing that there is always a choice to be made. The choice is either about which way to go or which door to choose—and more importantly, how you want to approach this choice inside yourself.

When change comes into your life, especially if it comes from the outside, many times you don't realize that you have the opportunity to make a choice about this change. You can feel, at least I did, that the change was forced upon you and that you were a victim. You might think to yourself: *I really feel stuck between a rock and a hard place. Because I feel like this change was unwanted. And NO, I don't want this.*

What I began to discover, through my own personal work and really opening up to learning new ways of working with myself, is that I did have a choice – I had a choice about how I was going to be with me while I faced the change.

In *Heaven* I talk about three areas where you can choose to take stock and make different choices. Although each area can have its challenges, still the choice is yours – you are deciding to review this relationship or situation for the possibility of making different choices.

But what about those changes that happen to you? Those changes that you did not ask for and want? Do you still have a choice to make?

For example, if the house that you're living in is being sold and you have to move, there's not a whole lot of wiggle room. You don't have a choice about moving or not. Or you were laid off from your job. Again, not your choice. But you do have a choice about how you want to approach this change.

What is the choice? Well, you can approach this change with anger, resentment, and fear, or you can approach this change with compassion, acceptance, and openness to new possibilities. THIS choice can shift a situation in your life—from something that is painful or fear based or full of anger and resentment—to a more compassionate, accepted, loving place inside of you.

I believe that when you shift your inner attitude and make THAT choice, it opens up the universe to assist you and move you into something that you didn't even know was there. Something good, something maybe even better.

Start to make different choices. And also be aware that there are always choices to be made.

THE HIDDEN PICTURE

When all you see is dots, soften your gaze, glimpse beyond them, and look for the hidden picture. Here is the object hidden in the Magic Eye image that appears on page 2.

NOTES

Part I: Glimpsing New Possibilities
Chapter 1: Turning Inward
1. Jo Coudert, *Advice from a Failure* (New York: Stein and Day, 1965), p. 131.

Chapter 4: The Power of Choice
1. David Whyte, excerpt from "The Truelove," *The House of Belonging* (Langley, WA: Many Rivers Press, 1997), p. 96.
2. William Wordsworth, "Ode: Intimations of Immortality from Recollections of Early Childhood," *Complete Poetical Works,* 1888 ed. (bartleby.com).

Part II: Recognizing Self-Limitations
Chapter 8: Seeing Only Lack
1. Trevor Leggett, "The Sieve," *Encounters in Yoga and Zen* (London, England: The Trevor Leggett Adhyatma Yoga Trust, 1982), p. 39.
2. Coleman Barks, trans., *The Essential Rumi* (Edison, NJ: Castle Books, 1997), p. 36.

Part III: Liberation
Chapter 15: Tuning In to Awareness
1. John-Roger, *Divine Essence* (Los Angeles: Mandeville Press, 1973), p. 149.

PERMISSIONS

I would like to thank the following for permission to reprint previously published material:

Magic Eye Inc.: Magic Eye image, viewing instructions, and hidden object. Copyright © 2000 by Magic Eye Inc. Reprinted by permission of Magic Eye Inc., http://www.magiceye.com

Stein and Day: Excerpt from *Advice from a Failure* by Jo Coudert. Copyright © 1965 by Jo Coudert. Reprinted by permission of the author.

Many Rivers Press: Excerpt from "The Truelove" in *The House of Belonging*. Copyright © 1997 by David Whyte. Reprinted by permission of the author.

Bartleby, Publisher: Excerpt from *Complete Poetical Works* by William Wordsworth. Reprinted by permission of Bartleby, Publisher.

The Trevor Leggett Adhyatma Yoga Trust: Excerpt from *Encounters in Yoga and Zen.* Copyright © 1982 by Trevor Leggett. Reprinted by permission of The Trevor Leggett Adhyatma Yoga Trust.

Castle Books: Excerpt from *The Essential Rumi.* Copyright © 1995 by Coleman Books. Reprinted by permission of Castle Books and Coleman Books.

Mandeville Press: *Excerpt from Divine Essence.* Copyright © 1973 by Peace Theological Seminary and College of Philosophy. Reprinted by permission of Mandeville Press.

To protect the privacy of people with whom I have worked, no anecdote in this book refers to any specific individual. Although illustrative material is presented, names, occupations, and identifying details have been altered. These composites of personal stories represent material collected by the author in her experience as a spiritual psychotherapist, counselor, teacher, colleague, and friend.

RESOURCES

To Order:

Amazon Author Page:
www.amazon.com/author/rebeccaeskeele

Rebecca's website:
www.RebeccaESkeele.com/author

More information about the Heaven on Earth Wisdom School and Rebecca's teachings:

Rebecca's membership site: Sacred Wisdom Teachings
www.RebeccaESkeele.com/membership

Rebecca's Youtube Channel
www.Youtube.com/rebeccaskeele

Let's Connect!

www.Facebook.com/rebecca.e.skeele

www.Linkedin.com/rebeccaskeele

Contact Rebecca:
www.RebeccaESkeele.com/contact